NEVIS
QUEEN OF THE CARIBBEAN

PHOTOGRAPHY BY JEROME DE BAECQUE

THIS BOOK HAS BEEN CONCEIVED AND PRODUCED BY:
BTP IMAGES - 10 RUE PERGOLESE - 75016 PARIS - FRANCE
TEL.: 45 00 35 55 - FAX: 45 00 36 62

CONTENTS

INTRODUCTION

by the Honorable Vance Amory, Premier of Nevis

As we celebrate our Tenth Anniversary of Independence, I welcome this opportunity to take a look at our homeland and her proud people through fresh eyes. Although her natural beauty and vitality are ever present, we can fully share in the excitement of discovery so evident in this pictorial introduction to Nevis. It presents to its readers a spectrum of the fauna and flora, the historical and modern landmarks, the work life and leisure activities which combine to portray the uniqueness of our island.

The authors are to be commended for capturing the essence, the special quality of Nevis.

Our island has had a very dramatic and colorful history. During the 18th and 19th centuries, it was one of the richest colonies of Great Britain and became, during that period, the playground of the rich and famous. There are stories of magnificent balls and parties which were staged at the Bath Hotel, that imposing structure overlooking the western segment of this lush and beautiful island. Visitors came not only for entertainment and socializing, but also to experience the rejuvenating waters of the hot volcanic springs.

This island has given rise to many tales of chivalry and romance. Lord Nelson and his illustrious deeds of bravery to preserve the sovereignty of the island for the British are well documented, and are part of our history. His courtship of and idyllic marriage to the Nevisian beauty, Fanny Nisbett, is a love story of international significance. Another native-born figure, Alexander Hamilton, became a colonel in the American Revolutionary Army and the first Secretary of the Treasury of the United States.

The sugarcane fields which covered the slopes of the island have long since disappeared, leaving the ruins of what were busy sugar mills and luxurious great houses. These are the remnants and the heritage of an era of prosperity when Nevis was known as the "Queen of the Caribbees". This book is a tribute to her former greatness, and a symbol of her potential for reclaiming a place of prominence in the Caribbean.

There are many attractive islands in the region which can lay claim to a glorious past, but none has the same capacity to charm, enchant and captivate its visitors at first sight. From the perfectly shaped cone of its cloud-capped mountain peak, sitting majestically at its center, down its slopes into the embrace of the Caribbean sea, one witnesses a calm and a beauty unmatched anywhere.

In more recent times, the island has experienced a new vigor as it is being rediscovered by those who

The Bath Hotel.

love romantic places. The small Plantation Inns with their cozy, homelike atmosphere, and the five-diamond Four Seasons Resort with its luxury and unsurpassed efficiency, provide a diversity of accommodations to satisfy the taste of the most discriminating visitor.

We, the people of Nevis, have an important part to play, both in preserving our legacy and in building an economy and a society in harmony with our traditions and aspirations. Our allies in this venture will find a spirit of open friendliness and cooperation.

It is my pleasure to have contributed to this most worthwhile effort, and I offer my congratulations to Mr. Jérôme de Baecque, and to all those who participated in the creation of this superb portrayal of Nevis, "Queen of the Caribbean".

GEOGRAPHY

by Laure Mansuy and Deborah Lellouch

LOCATION

The island of Nevis belongs to the Leeward Islands of the West Indies archipelago and is one of a chain of relatively young volcanic islands stretching from Saba to Grenada.

At a latitude of 17°10′ and a longitude of 62°35′, Nevis is located two miles southeast of St Kitts. A channel called "the Narrows", notorious for its rough seas, separates the two islands. Its bottom is covered with magnificient coral reefs. The perimeter of this small island paradise is bordered by long stretches of sandy beach broken by occasional rocky promontories.

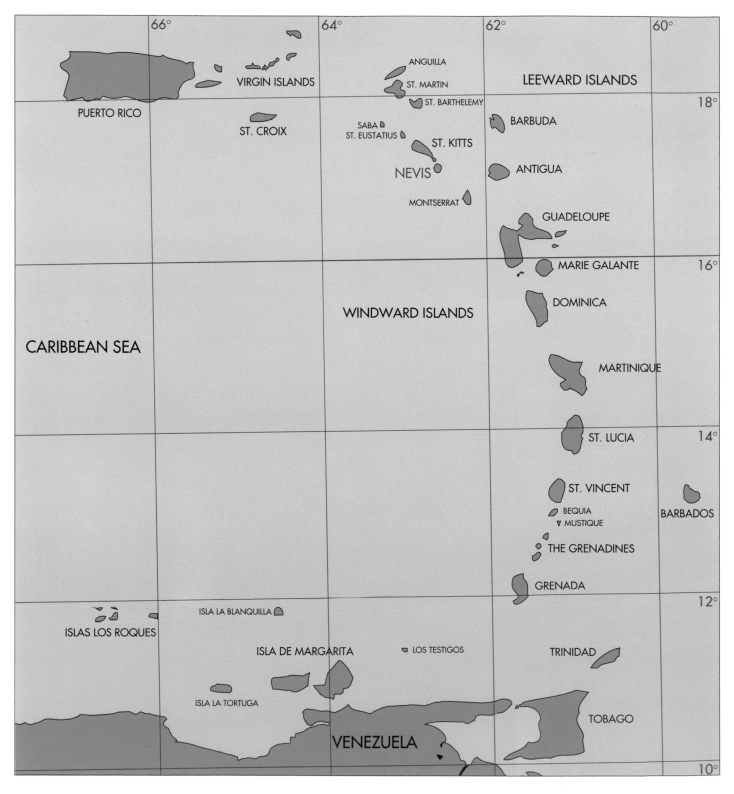

TOPOGRAGHY AND GEOLOGY

The island is dominated by a central volcanic cone, Nevis Peak, whose cloud-crowned summit rises to a height of 3,232 feet (985 meters). The form of the island is nearly circular, covering an area of 36 square miles (92 square kilometers). Windy Hill to the north and Saddle Hill to the south line up with Nevis Peak to form a NNW/SSE watershed. Geologists have identified many types of volcanic and sedimentary rocks which, under the influence of various microclimates, have evolved into a great diversity of soils rich in mineral elements required by plants. Many of these, however, are considered to have little agronomic value due to insufficient drainage and the presence of volcanic boulders which inhibits the development of mechanized agriculture.

CLIMATE

Located 6° south of the Tropic of Cancer, Nevis is characterized by a tropical and maritime climate, strongly influenced by steady Northeasterlies. There is a wide range of microclimates which vary greatly with height, location and orientation.

Tradewinds break against Nevis Peak, creating orogenic cloud formations which rarely dissipate. Annual rainfall averages 46 inches (1,170 milimeters) at sea level.

The climate is remarkable, even by Caribbean standards. Sunshine is guaranteed virtually every day of the year. Temperatures average 78° Fahrenheit (25° centigrade) year 'round. There is a constant cooling breeze from the sea, and humidity is very low. There is no rainy season as such, but short and heavy rainshowers occur from July to January. Tropical storm activity is carefully monitored in the region, and advisories are broadcast via the Weather Channel from June through November.

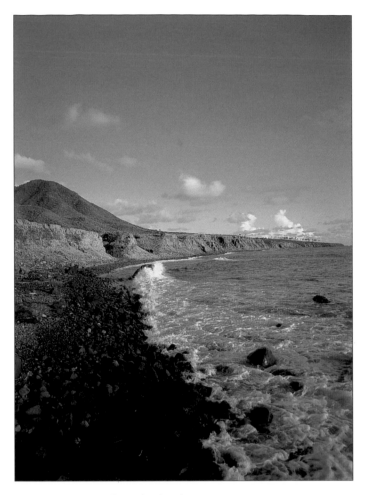

The rocky shoreline at New River.

VEGETATION

The present vegetation has evolved as a result of both human activity and climatic conditions. Above an altitude of 1,300 feet (400 meters), Nevis Island is covered with an evergreen tropical forest. Only a faint light penetrates the thick and luxuriant leaves, creepers and vines, while the ground is entirely covered with ferns.

Near the summit of Nevis Peak, this exuberant forest tends to disappear and is gradually replaced by gnarled shrubs, moss, and magnificent clusters of orchids.

What is left of the original jungle can be found above Jessups on the northwestern slopes of Nevis Peak, where the high and dense canopy of leaves remains undamaged. Dominant species are mountain cabbage palms (Euterpe globosa) gumlins (Dacryodes excelsa) and burrwood (Slonea truncata).

Below 1,300 feet (400 meters), very little of the original vegetation is left, as farm land and a golf course occupy most of the remaining surface. A littoral belt of vegetation, resistant to the salty ocean spray, serves a vital function in preventing the erosion of sand and soil.

Salt and fresh water mix in swamps along the coast; mangrove trees grow in these shallow waters, and provide a sanctuary for many species of migrant birds.

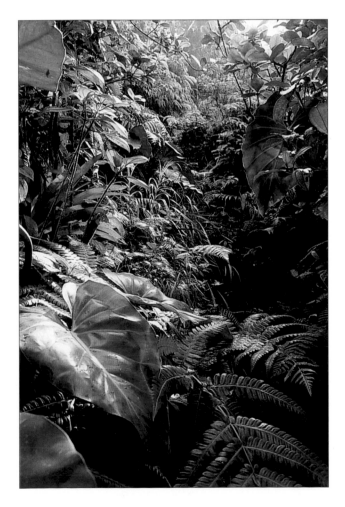

The luxuriant vegetation in the rain-forest.

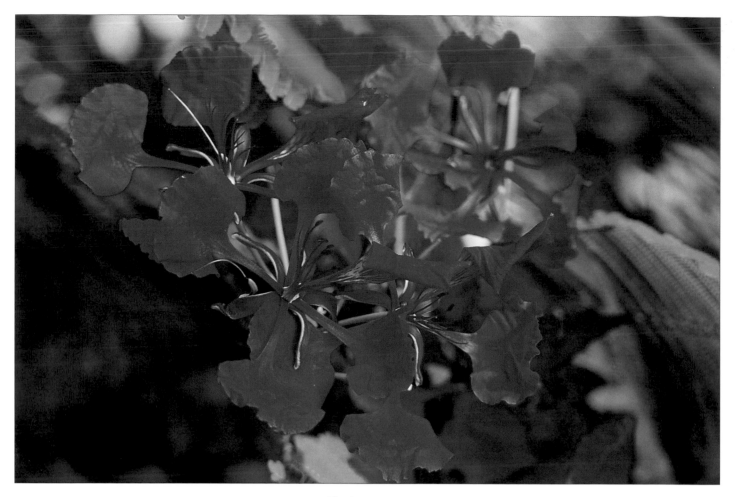

Flamboyant tree.

FLORA

The island is a veritable Garden of Eden, of interest to botanists and amateurs alike.

In the wild, or in parks and private gardens, an infinite diversity of tropical flora can be admired all year 'round:. Magenta bougainvilleas, pink or white oleanders, variegated hibiscus, vermillion flamboyants, yellow allamandas... The air is balmy with the scent of the flowering frangipani trees. In the plains area, Royal palms and coconut trees grow everywhere. Easy-to-reach avocados, bananas, breadfruit, mangos, papayas and citrus fruits are staples of the Nevisian diet.

Hibiscus.

Papaya tree.

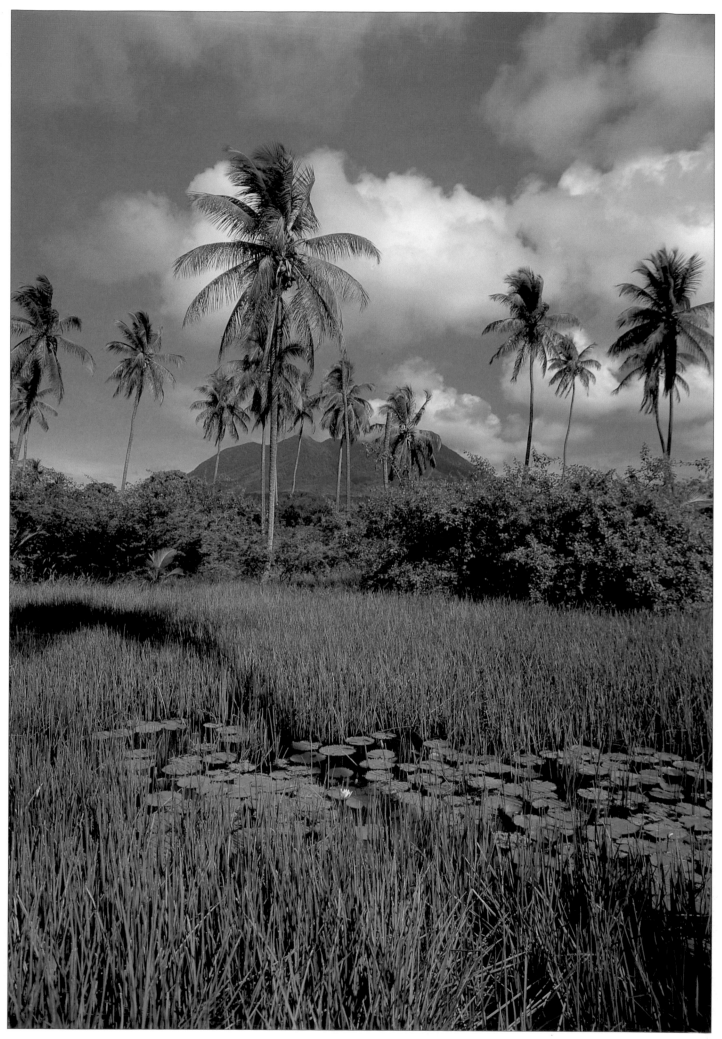

Coconut grove at Nelson's Spring.

Domesticated donkey.

Great white heron.

FAUNA

The fauna, typical of the Caribbean, consists of small and innofensive mammals, lizards, birds, and aquatic creatures, many of which arrived on the island aboard seagoing vessels. The Vervet Monkey, playful and gregarious, inhabits the lush forest areas, feeding on mangos and papayas, often stolen from nearby gardens. Some of the best spots for observing "monkey business" are the ghauts leading down from the Golden Rock Estate where, at dawn and dusk, they can be seen in family groups. Frequent visitors to the outdoor restaurants include "sugar birds" and tiny lizards, searching for crumbs and tidbits. Birds come in all colors and sizes, from the green-throated carib to the great white heron. Minute crested humming-birds drink nectar from deep-throated ginger blossoms. The brown pelican, national symbol and fisherman, *par excellence*, can be seen diving after schools of flying fish near the coast. Farmyard animals are part of the landscape, and of the microeconomy of the island. The sea fauna is rich. Along the shore, crabs, conch, lobsters and nesting sea turtles can be seen by those who enjoy snorkling. Deep-sea fishing with seasoned professionals offers the opportunity to catch swordfish, wahoo and even sharks. There are no snakes, and the rare insect bites recorded are non-lethal. Nevis, in all its splendor, affords the visitor a rare opportunity to commune with nature.

Red dragonfly.

Green lizard.

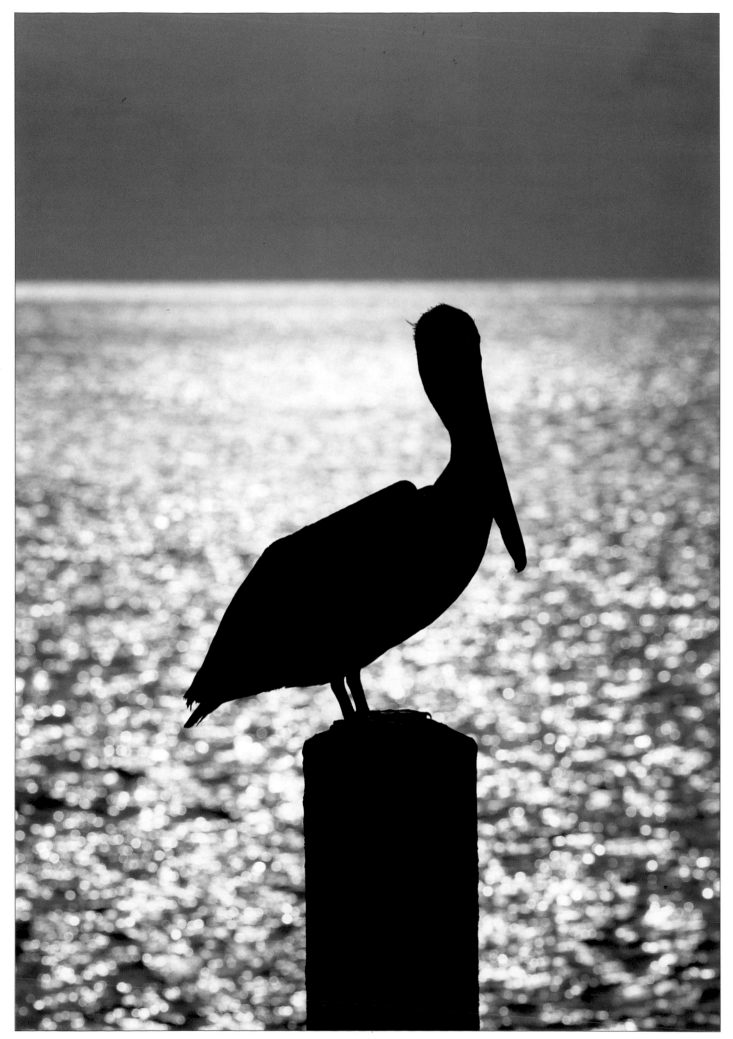

Brown pelican.

HISTORY OF NEVIS

By Vincent K. Hubbard,
Author of <u>Swords, Ships and Sugar: a History of Nevis to 1900</u>

The first human inhabitants of Nevis were pre-ceramic Indians called Sibonay. They are believed to have come to Nevis around 2,000 years ago from Central America, but the place of their origin is not certain. At any rate, all that remains of them here are a few primitive stone or shell tools. They were followed by Arawak Indians, who came from the Orinoco River Basin in Venezuela. The Carib Indians, who came from the same general area of South America, arrived several hundred years later. There are 22 known Indian sites in Nevis, marked with sherds of pottery, pieces of flint stone, and shell heaps. From time to time human bones are found when erosion exposes them. Archaeologists estimate that, between 500 and 600 A.D., the Indian population of Nevis was anywhere from 1,000 to 5,000.

Nevis and all the Leeward Islands were designated "useless islands" by Spain, which claimed the entire Caribbean from the time of Columbus' second voyage to 1671. Columbus officially claimed Nevis (originally named St. Martin) on 11 November 1493, when he anchored overnight off the west coast of the island. Within 50 years of Columbus' voyage, the name of the island appeared on maps as "Nieves", the Spanish word for snow. The clouds around the mountain peak evidently looked like a snow cap to early sailors.

The Spanish Crown allowed the taking of Carib Indians as slaves, because they were cannibals, but not the Arawaks. It was not then and is not now clear what differences there were between the two peoples. The near elimination of the Indian population of both Nevis and the Caribbean by Spanish slave raids, and the spread of European diseases unwittingly carried by them, is one of the most tragic chapters in human history. By 1600, there were only a handful of Indians left in Nevis, if indeed there were any permanent Indian residents here. It was noted by an 18th-century writer that the remaining Indians were expelled from Nevis, St. Kitts and Antigua in 1640; but, in 1680, a census of Nevis indicated there were a few still working as slaves on Nevis plantations.

A general view of the island from the west side.

The Newcastle Redoubt, almost certainly the oldest standing building in the Commonwealth Caribbean, was constructed as protection against Indian raids. The date of its building was very likely before 1640, and it is shown on a French military intelligence map drawn in 1703. It is noted that no cannon were mounted in it, which indicates it was outdated even at that early time. The building could not withstand an attack by European artillery, as the door opening faces the sea whence ships could easily fire into it. The building is only seven meters square. On the lower level are two musket slits per wall, and on the upper level are two large holes per wall where a small 3 or 4-pounder gun on a moveable carriage could be used to fire grapeshot at attackers.

The earliest written record of a visit to Nevis was in 1603, by Captain Bartholemew Gilbert, of Plymouth, England. He does not mention seeing any Indians here. The purpose of his trip was to harvest *lignum vitae* logs. This wood, no longer found in Nevis, was so heavy it would not float and so hard termites could not eat it. It was sometimes used for industrial gear wheels in place of iron. Gilbert commented that sea turtles were abundant, and some were so large that a single one fed his 24 men for three days.

In 1607, Captain John Smith and his men stopped for five days in Nevis on their way to found the colony of Virginia in North America. He wrote that he established a carefully-guarded camp in case of Indian attack, and his men encountered an Indian hunting party inland, but both groups ran from each other and there was no confrontation. Smith remarked that Nevis was completely wooded from the edge of the sea to the top of the mountain, and that there was a hot water spring (the Bath Spring) whose waters would cure gunpowder burns and serious skin irritations. A 1608 visitor declared those waters could cure leprosy and coughs as well. This spring still exists on the grounds of the ruins of the Bath Hotel, built in 1778, as the first resort hotel in the Caribbean.

The Bath Spring was famous among early European explorers in the Caribbean, and Nevis became a common stopover, especially for English and Dutch ships passing through the area on their way to North America. Spain claimed all the islands for themselves, and their navy was so powerful that the Caribbean was termed "a Spanish lake" in the 16th and 17th centuries. Any non-Spanish vessels venturing into it did so at their peril.

In 1620, an incident occurred on the west coast of Nevis in which two Spanish men-of-war, one of 16 and the other of 20 guns and both disguised to look like Dutch merchant ships, lay in wait for trespassers. A small English merchantman on her way to Virginia, the eight-gun *Margaret and John* of London, stopped at Nevis for fresh water. She carried 109 people on board, mostly migrating families, and six French sailors who had been shipwrecked in Martinique for six months and had lived with the Indians. The Frenchmen warned the English Captain that they had seen two Spanish warships in Martinique earlier, and they believed the vessels anchored in Nevis were the very same ones.

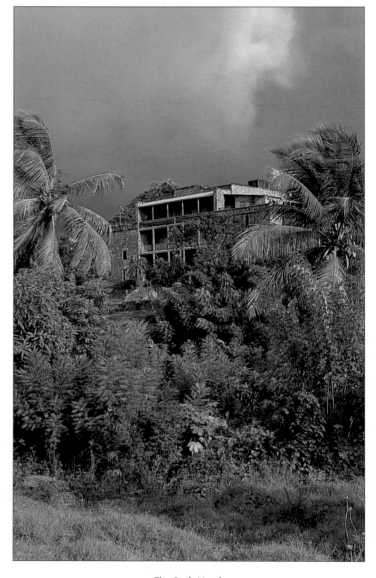

A longboat was sent out to hail the unidentified ships. When the sailors determined the vessels were indeed Spanish, they came about and raced back toward *Margaret and John* at full speed. The warships immediately ran up the Spanish flag and opened fire on the longboat with muskets and swivel cannon. One man reported a ball passed through his jacket and the bottom of the boat, and he plugged up the hole with his handkerchief.
Margaret and John attempted to escape but her anchor had fouled on the bottom and could not be raised. Helpless, she was attacked by one Spanish warship which came alongside, fired a broadside into her, and attempted a boarding. After a brutal hand-to-hand fight on the deck, the attackers were driven off. The Spanish Captain was killed leading his men over the rail. Nineteen men were killed on *Margaret and John*, including three of the French sailors, before the anchor cable was cut and she managed to escape.

This small battle was indicative of the ongoing conflicts between European powers which would later engulf Nevis. Literally, the Caribbean would be the anvil for European wars until the mid-19th century. In 1625, Nevis was unofficially settled by Englishmen coming from St.Kitts. Officially, it was settled in 1628, and the first Governor of Nevis then proceeded to steal the island's first tobacco crop.

The Bath Hotel.

His career was cut short when Nevis was invaded by the Spanish in 1629, and the tiny settlement was destroyed and the settlers dispersed. Much of the land-clearing, dangerous and difficult work, was being done by indentured Irish Roman Catholic servants who disliked the Protestant English, joined the Spanish invaders, and left Nevis for good.

The first European immigrants to the island were usually indentured for a period of three to five years and were, in effect, contract slaves. They would exchange their labor for a term to a person paying their passage across the sea, and these contracts could be bought and sold. Europeans found it difficult to adjust to the heat; their diet was poor, and the resulting death rate was so high that fewer than half of them lived to see the end of their indenture periods. Male indentured servants exceeded female by a three-to-one ratio, and, as a result, there was chronic drunkeness and fighting among them. However, those who finished their indentures were usually able to obtain land and became small farmers.

The first commercial enterprise on Nevis was small farming of cotton, tobacco, indigo, and vegetables. The cultivation of sugar cane and the ability to crystallize it (a secret brought by Dutch traders and Jewish emigrants from Brazil) changed the island completely. By 1642, Nevis was acknowledged to produce the finest sugar in the Caribbean, and its population was estimated to be 10,000, when Virginia had a population of only 8,000. It was noted, in 1727, that one gallon of cane juice from Nevis produced 24 ounces of sugar, when the average in the Caribbean was only 16 ounces per gallon. For a time, Nevis became fabulously rich from sugar.

Sugarmill at work.

Sugar production was, however, a labor-intensive process, and European labor became difficult to obtain because of the very high death rate in the Caribbean. At that point, the importation of African slave labor commenced. As with the indentured servants, their death rate was extremely high. It was estimated that about 22% would die on the "middle passage" voyage from Africa to Nevis, and approximately two-fifths of those who survived the trip died becoming "seasoned" to life here. Nevis reached the height of its prosperity in the last quarter of the 17th century. It was the richest Caribbean island, save Barbados. In 1675, Nevis became the depot for the slave trade for all the Leeward Islands. The average number of slaves passing through Nevis in that era was from 6,000 to 11,000 annually. Nevis planters naturally selected the best slaves for themselves, much to the distress of planters on the other islands.

This prosperity was achieved in spite of almost constant warfare and the natural devastations of hurricanes and earthquakes. Several times in the 17th century, Nevis barely avoided being taken by the French and Dutch. In 1667, France very nearly took all the Leeward Islands from England. St. Kitts, Montserrat and Antigua were captured one by one, and only Nevis, the richest, most populous and best fortified, remained in English hands. In 1666, a French attack was repelled, and, had a follow-up attack been made with stronger forces, Nevis probably would have been captured. Nearly 5,000 refugees from other islands had fallen back to Nevis, and food and military ordnance were in very short supply.

West Indies Governor Lord Willoughby, in Barbados, realized it was essential to Great Britain that Nevis be held. He gathered a fleet of 17 ships, 1,000 troops, 2,000 muskets, and supplies of food and military ordnance, and sailed to the relief of Nevis. He never made it. On 18 July 1667, a massive hurricane caught his fleet off Guadeloupe. Every single ship was lost, and Lord Willoughby and 1,500 men were drowned. Bodies and wreckage of his ships washed ashore throughout the Leewards. Nevis itself was devastated by the hurricane. The inhabitants had to leave their collapsing houses and throw themselves flat on the ground in open fields to survive. Had the French been able to mount an attack, Nevis undoubtedly would have fallen; but the French islands had been hit by the storm as well, and it was not possible for them to send troops to Nevis for some months.

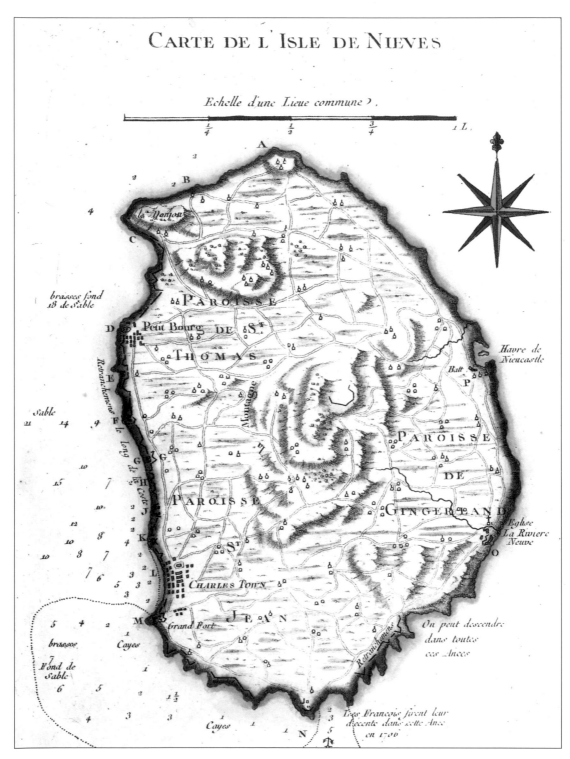

A French map dating from the 18th Century.

The French prepared a careful plan for an invasion of Nevis. A combined Franco-Dutch fleet of 30 ships was assembled in Guadeloupe under the overall command of General de la Barre. Sixteen were French men-of-war, ranging in size from 20 to 38 guns, and three were Dutch men-of-war under the command of Admiral de Crynsens, two of 28 guns and one of 38 guns. The remainder of the vessels were supply ships and troop carriers. The Carib Indians were allied with the French as well and the Indians arrived on the east side of Nevis in a fleet of large war canoes carrying 30 to 40 warriors per vessel. If the French and Dutch landed on the western side of the island, the Caribs would take their shallow draft canoes over the reefs and attack on the eastern side. The militia could not defend both sides of the island at once. It was a very sound plan.

The British, however, had dispatched ten warships carrying desperately-needed supplies to Nevis, under the command of Captain (later Admiral) Sir John Berry, "an expert seaman and a courageous, bold commander". Berry's flagship was the HMS Coronation, a powerful 50-gun ship of the line. The Franco-Dutch fleet was detected approaching Nevis, and Berry launched an immediate attack against the larger fleet. He "had the weather gauge" in his favor, meaning the wind was astern of his ships. De la Barre was not a naval commander, and could not decide whether to stand and fight Berry or protect his supply ships; and, therefore, he did not meet Berry's attack forcefully, as the Dutch Admiral urged him to do.

The battle raged for four hours. In the thick of the fight, off the southwest coast of Nevis, one of Berry's warships blew up and sank with heavy loss of life. Admiral de Crynsens then moved to engage Coronation with all three of his men-of-war, and the battle turned in favor of the combined fleet. However, Berry ordered that a fireship be sent against de Crynsens' vessels, which forced them to bear off before his flagship was heavily damaged, and the tide of battle turned in his favor once again. At last, De la Barre broke off action and withdrew to St. Kitts, giving Berry a victory and ultimately enabling Britain to retain all the Leewards. The Caribs quickly departed following the engagement.

In 1673, the Dutch attacked Nevis with 15 ships and 1,100 men, hoping to land troops and capture the island. During the attack, the Dutch ships received such a pounding from Nevis' shore batteries that onshore observers noted sailors going over the sides with wooden plugs to stop up leaks caused by cannonballs. Not only were the Dutch unable to land troops, they were not even able to take any merchant ships as prizes, although they tried repeatedly.

The years 1689 and 1690 were devastating for Nevis. During those years, successive epidemics of fever, ague, and bloody flux killed nearly half of the population. Nevis went from being the strongest of the Leewards to the weakest, and a terrible earthquake, in 1690, caused all the brick and stone buildings to "drop of a sudden from top to bottom in perfect ruins". However, in spite of natural and man-made calamities, Nevis continued to grow more and more prosperous.

Fort Charles.

In 1671, construction of Fort Charles began. In that year the Leeward Islands became a separate colony and wealthy Nevis was its seat. It remained so for over 50 years. The fort was completed within the decade by slave labor and mounted 26 cannon. Combined with nine other batteries on the Leeward side of the island, Nevis was very well protected, and Charlestown was then considered the best fortified harbor in the Caribbean. Even before the fort was finished, the Dutch tested it with an attack. Its guns were continually used against pirate attacks and those of other enemies, usually the French.

In those years, there was a protocol in effect that required a foreign ship entering the harbor to strike its colors. In response, the shore batteries would fire a blank cannon salute. The purpose was to show that the two nations were not at war. If a vessel failed to strike, a shot would be fired from land across her bows as a warning. If she did not then strike, worse would follow. In 1679, a small French merchantman named La Sara de Rochelle entered Charlestown harbor and failed to strike her colors. A warning shot was duly fired from Fort Charles. Captain Michel, "the impudent fellow", as the Governor called him, responded by firing a cannon at the British flag flying over the Fort. This action resulted in angry return fire from the fort, which missed its target. Captain Michel bore off to French St. Kitts, but left Nevis Governor Sir William Stapleton infuriated. Stapleton wrote to England: "It frets me to skin and bones to see such indignities heaped on the King's flag by their very merchantmen."

In 1700, a similar occurrence took place which had more serious and long-lasting consequences. French Admiral de Modene arrived in Charlestown with three powerful ships of the line. His visit was expected, and the nations were at peace, but he failed to strike his colors. As he anchored, a warning shot was fired across his bows from Fort Charles. A longboat was sent from shore to determine why he had not lowered his flag as protocol demanded. Evidently very much offended, de Modene apologized and promised to strike. He further declared that, after the salute was fired from the fort, he would fire a salute to England from his warship's guns as an act of contrition.

The cannon at Fort Charles had been loaded with shot, but it was removed; and, at the appointed time, the fort's guns fired their blank salute. De Modene, however, ordered all the guns of his three vessels to be fully loaded, and, rather than firing a blank salute, his flagship fired a full broadside into the fort and his other two ships fired broadside after broadside into Charlestown. People of every station of life had gathered on the bayfront to witness this military spectacle, and many were killed or wounded by shot. Several English merchantmen, anchored in the harbor, responded by firing at the French warships with their small cannon, but were battered into submission before their guns had any effect. De Modene sailed away leaving much damage in the town and an abiding distrust of the French, by the entire population, which would manifest itself in 1706, when England and France were once again at war.

The war of the Spanish succession began in 1703, and pitted Great Britain and Holland against France and Spain. The results were soon felt in the Caribbean. In February 1706, a French fleet under the command of Admiral Count de Chauvanac attacked Nevis with 24 ships and 1,100 troops. They anchored off Cades Bay and Pinney's Beach on the western side of the island and attempted to land troops. The attack was expected. Four hundred and thirty Nevis militia and 125 British regulars, brought from Antigua under the command of Governor John Johnson, were waiting. Their strong resistance, combined with heavy seas, prevented a French landing for five days, despite repeated attempts. Count de Chauvanac gave up the attempt, but went on to poorly-prepared St. Kitts, captured it in a single day, and spent three days plundering it. Over 600 slaves were taken from St. Kitts and much damage was done.

Rich Nevis, however, remained the prime target of the French. In March 1706, with their forces increased to 36 ships and 2,100 troops, the French, under the command of Pierre Le Moyne d'Iberville, the founder of Louisiana in North America, approached Nevis a second time. This attack was much better planned. D'Iberville approached from the South, and sailed around the eastern side of the island with the main body of his fleet, but he left six supply vessels anchored off the south side of Nevis. These vessels were ignored by the Nevis land commander, as they were not warships–a great mistake. D'Iberville had secreted himself and 900 troops on board. The main fleet circled the island and anchored off the western beaches at approximately the same place as before. At dawn on Good Friday, the warships opened fire on the shore batteries with a thunderous bombardment. However, this time Governor Johnson and the 125 regulars were in Antigua, and only 430 militia opposed them on the beaches.

Fort Charles's cannon.

D'Iberville, hearing the distant cannon fire, immediately landed his 900 troops unopposed and marched North towards Charlestown. They were soon discovered, but only a handful of militia were available to oppose them. The militia fought bravely, but were quickly overwhelmed in spite of assistance from Fort Charles's cannon. The fort was then taken when d'Iberville's troops forced the landward entrance. When the fort fell, 22 British merchant ships in Charlestown harbor lost their protection, and all were captured. The French troops marched from there into Charlestown, where they plundered and fired the town. The rest of the Nevis militia retreated from the beaches and headed for a mountain redoubt, where they could withstand a siege. D'Iberville's forces pressed them on the retreat, and a battle occurred at Morning Star Plantation where the outnumbered militia were again defeated.

Slaves working in the sugar cane fields.

The militia made their way to the redoubt, where they were in a strong defensive position. However, in an "ignominious" surrender, they capitulated the next morning without firing a shot. Nevis had fallen in three days to d'Iberville's well-planned and executed attack, and his troops systematically began to pillage the island. The slaves, however, did not give up. Thirty-four hundred were captured initially and subsequently transported to Martinique, but about 1,000 more, poorly armed and militarily untrained, made their way up Mount Nevis and established a defensive position. When French troops advanced to attack, they were driven back, time and again, by "murderous fire". It was written by an English militiaman that the slaves' "brave behavior and defense there shamed what some of their masters did, and they do not shrink to tell us so". The slaves held 18 days until the French left the island, mistakenly believing that a British fleet was approaching. It is likely that Admiral de Modene's action, in 1700, encouraged them to take such a strong stand in 1706.

Angered by the slaves' unexpected resistance, d'Iberville demanded that the planters turn over 1,400 more slaves or pay a tribute of 30 pounds per slave; and, to enforce his demand, he took three leading planters hostage and carried them to Martinique, where they languished in prison until 1715.

Nevis was devastated by this savage attack. In 1704, its sugar production had been 2,965 tons, but it plunged to only 533 tons in 1706. The 1704 figures would not be equalled again for eighty years. The British Parliament voted 100,000 pounds in aid for Nevis, but that was only a tenth of the island's losses. The sad fact was that Nevis would never fully recover, and its economy began a decline which would continue until its almost total failure in the 1920's and 1930's.

A windmill in function.

Chargement of boats.

The 18th century was a difficult one for Nevis. Twenty-six hurricanes would strike the island with devastating results. In 1725 and 1726, starvation threatened because of drought. An incipient slave rebellion was discovered in 1725, but stopped before violence could occur when two of the alleged leaders were captured by the militia and burned alive. The overall population declined and the percentage of Europeans fell from one-quarter of the population to one-tenth during that century. As the fertility of the soil declined from exhaustion and erosion, more slaves were required to manure and prepare the land in order to maintain the same level of sugar production. Sugar prices remained high because of growing demand in Europe, but the cost of production in Nevis increased, and the profit margin for planters narrowed. Slaves frequently suffered from lack of food and the poor nutritional content of food they did receive. Sugar was so valuable that the land available for planting food crops shrank. It was more economical to grow sugar, sell it to Britain, and buy food products in bulk from North America.

This trade system would come to a halt with the American Revolution. Food imports from the 13 rebellious colonies stopped entirely during the war, which lasted from 1776 to 1783. Three to four hundred slaves starved to death in Nevis, and many more were so weakened by malnutrition that they had low resistance to disease and died of natural causes. A Nevis planter wrote to England in 1777, that because of the war, he would "go bankrupt or starve to death, or both". This very nearly came true.

West Indian planters on the whole, were sympathetic to the North American rebels, and, had they had the power to do so, would probably have joined them. By 1776, the Nevis economy had generally recovered from the 1706 disaster, but she had been left behind in development by the other Leewards, and had become the poorest and least productive of them all. What struck immediate fear into Nevis, was the entry of France on the American side of the war in 1778. Shortly afterward, Spain and Holland followed. British sea power was drawn off to North America, and the Caribbean was wide open to Britain's enemies. Nevis attempted to rebuild its defenses, but lacked the funds to do so effectively.

French Admiral Count d'Estaing.

The first enemy contact was with a 38-vessel warfleet under the command of French Admiral Count d'Estaing, which was blockading Charlestown Harbor in September 1779. Nature came to Nevis' rescue, when a hurricane slammed into the island and d'Estaing's fleet on 4 September, sinking several of his ships, damaging the rest, and causing him to withdraw from the Caribbean. His lost ships have never been found.

Events remained reasonably calm until 1782. Early that year, a 28-gun British frigate, *HMS Solebay*, was being pursued by three French warships, and was desperately attempting to reach the protection of Nevis's shore batteries, when she ran aground on a reef off the southern coast of the island. The French ships began firing into her as she lay aground; and, rather than lose her, the captain ordered her burned, and escaped to shore in longboats with the entire crew. When the fire reached her powder magazine, she blew up.

Only a week later, a column of nearly 50 ships was sighted standing for the island, led by Admiral Count François de Grasse, in the 130-gun ship of the line *Ville de Paris*, the most powerful warship on earth. De Grasse and his fleet made for Fort Charles, passing within range of her cannon, but going on to anchor in St. Kitts. De Grasse held his fire, and the gunners at Fort Charles wisely did the same, knowing that the fleet could easily destroy the fort if fighting broke out. De Grasse carried an invasion force of over 5,000 to St. Kitts in order to take Brimstone Hill, "The Gibraltar of the Caribbean". The British were losing the war in North America, and, if Brimstone Hill fell, all the British West India colonies might be lost to them as well.

The 130-gun ship Ville de Paris.

A necessary part of this plan was keeping Nevis in French hands while Brimstone Hill was besieged. De Grasse sent a warship to Nevis, demanding its surrender. With only 300 militia available, and many worn cannon in her forts, Nevis had no choice but to surrender. De Grasse gave very generous terms. After being presented with "ten fat sheep" by the President of the Nevis Council, de Grasse stated that additional gifts of food would displease him, as he would be forced to refuse them. He could see that Nevis was so impoverished that it could not afford to give up any edibles. He wrote to the President: "I am much affected at the scarcity which your island finds itself in for the support of your negroes".

A small garrison of French troops, under the command of Lieutenant Millon de Villeroy, was placed in Fort Charles. The original number was to have been only six men, but at the request of President Herbert of the Nevis Council, the size was increased. Herbert wrote de Grasse that he feared the slaves would rise against a small French force, especially if English ships appeared. De Grasse agreed, and sent a warship to take all of Nevis's good cannon to use at Brimstone Hill against the English. After 35 days of fighting, Brimstone Hill fell. Very shortly afterwards, the Treaty of Versailles was signed, and Nevis returned to British rule.

In 1787, Captain Horatio Nelson of the Royal Navy, was dispatched to the West Indies. His first assignment was to enforce the British Navigation Acts in Nevis, which he did with customary vigor. He seized three American vessels flying the British flag, illegally, and impounded their cargoes. The cargoes belonged to Nevis merchants, who promptly sued Nelson. The suit was decided in Nelson's favor, and the man who assisted him, President Herbert of the Nevis Council, introduced Nelson to his young widowed niece, Frances Herbert Nisbett. Shortly afterward, the two were married at Montpellier Plantation, with the Duke of Clarence, later King William IV, acting as Nelson's best man. The night before the wedding, a band of hungry runaway slaves stole the ox being fattened for the wedding feast, and ate it themselves.

Admiral, Viscount Nelson, Duke of Bronte.

The United States became a major trading partner with the West Indies after the Revolutionary War. Alexander Hamilton, born in Nevis in 1757, was instrumental in the American victory and became the first Secretary of the Treasury of the United States. As such, he kept an eye on American trade with his birthplace. The Department of the Navy was formed in 1795, and three medium-sized frigates were built. This navy had not only never won an engagement, it had never even fought a battle. In 1799, the United States and France became involved in a undeclared war. One of the three frigates, the 38-gun *USS Constellation*, was dispatched to the West Indies to protect American shipping from French commerce raiders.

On 9 February 1799, *Constellation* was patrolling north of Nevis, when another warship was sighted. She was the 40-gun French frigate *L'Insurgente*, the most daring and dangerous of the French raiders. She had already captured six American merchant vessels. *Constellation* challenged her and set off in pursuit, when she changed course and made for the neutral Dutch island of Saba. The chase lasted three hours, during which time the French ship was struck by a rain squall and lost her main topmast. This slowed *L'Insurgente* and hampered her agility. *Constellation* overtook her about a mile and a half off the southeast coast of Nevis. With all her guns bearing, she fired a broadside into *L'Insurgente*, which returned fire at once. Except for the damage to *L'Insurgente*, the vessels were evenly matched and battled furiously for an hour and a half, at which time *L'Insurgente* struck her colors and surrendered. Nevis was the site, not only of the first United States naval battle, but of its first victory as well.

The 19th century in Nevis saw Emancipation, the end of military activity and failure of the sugar economy. Two more attacks were made upon Nevis by French forces: one in 1805, and another in 1806, led by Jerome Bonaparte. That was the last military offensive to be made against the island.

The militia was disbanded in 1838, and the forts were abandoned in 1854. Economic decline and growing American power put an end to European colonial adventures in the Caribbean.

In spite of increased demand for sugar, Europe and North America, by the 1820's produced much of their own needs, and new sugar producing colonies in the British Empire drove prices steadily downward. Emancipation brought freedom to 8,815 slaves in Nevis, and compensation of 151,006 pounds to their masters. The slaves received nothing for their years of servitude, and faced a steadily deteriorating economic situation. The average wage for a laborer in Nevis was five pence per day, at a time when it cost four pence per day to feed a prisoner in an English jail. The result was a mass migration outward, and a subsequent decline in population.

The economy staggered on until the 1890's, when the situation suddenly worsened. The Nevis sugar industry picked up during World War I, but collapsed almost totally in the 1920's and 1930's, when estates were abandoned and the government confiscated them for non-payment of taxes. Some of the steam mills continued to crush cane in small amounts; the last ceased operation in 1958. In 1883, the Nevis government was abolished and amalgamated with St. Kitts. For the first time in 258 years, Nevis no longer had a local government. This situation remained until 1983, when the Nevis Assembly was reconstituted and local self-government returned.

By the 1930's, the Caribbean was considered an "Imperial Slum" – a far cry from the 1770's, when Willam Pitt declared that four–fifths of Britain's overseas wealth derived from the West Indies. Britain belatedly recognized its obligation to the region in the 1930's, when agitation for better living and working conditions began to surface, and West Indians began speaking out. The Moyne Commission was established, and sent to the Caribbean to assess the situation and make recommendations for improving living conditions. It visited Nevis on its tour. Many recommendations were delayed in implementation by World War II, but its most significant and long-lasting contribution was in the area of public health. The mosquito-borne diseases of yellow fever and malaria were eliminated, and health conditions and life expectancy improved dramatically.

During World War II, enough money was voluntarily collected in St.Kitts and Nevis to purchase two spitfires for the RAF during the Battle of Britain. Nevis sent a number of men to serve in the British armed forces. Conditions were very hard in Nevis during the war years. Flour, especially, was in very short supply. In the years after the war, it was noted, that only five Europeans were resident in Nevis. An attempt was made during the 1950's to replace sugar with coconut and cotton production, but met with only limited success.

Even though money was always in short supply in the 19th century, the Methodist and Anglican churches established church schools, and attendance was rigorously enforced. When government took over the education system, its excellence continued. In Nevis, approximately 22% of revenue is spent on schools; the largest single item in the island's budget. The success of this approach is evident in the Federation's literacy rate of 98%, the highest in the western hemisphere.

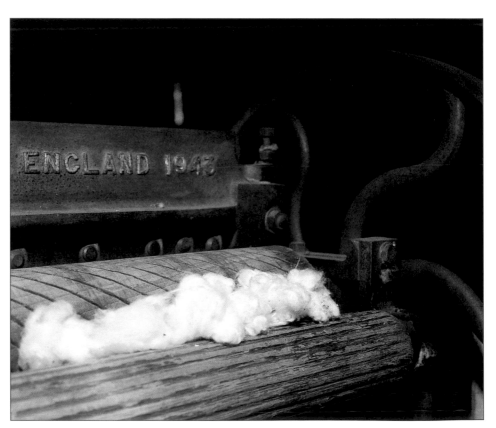

Cotton Gin.

In 1970, a tragedy occurred which affected almost every family in Nevis. Returning from Basseterre, the ferry M.V. *Christena* sank off Nag's Head. It was badly overloaded, and began taking water rapidly in the channel. Before any orderly evacuation could be accomplished, it started sinking by the stern, and, as it went down, capsized, trapping passengers inside. Many occupants were unable to reach life preservers, and 209 people drowned. Valiant efforts were made by boats in the area to pick up survivors, but the suddenness of the accident and the numbers of people involved, made substantial rescue impossible. A plaque in the Gingerland Methodist Church gives the names of 14 church members who perished in the accident, and illustrates how the tragedy touched the entire island.

In the 1960's, Britain created the Federation of St.Kitts, Nevis and Anguilla and granted it limited self-government. The seat of the Federation was in St.Kitts, and Robert L.Bradshaw was elected the first Prime Minister. Anguilla soon left the Federation and Nevis has the constitutional right, on a two-thirds public referendum, to leave the Federation and become independent should it choose to do so. On 19 September 1983, the Federation became independent of Great Britain and joined the Commonwealth.

National Flag of St. Kitts and Nevis.

Since the Federation was created and independence granted, prosperity is returning to Nevis after many long and painful years of relative poverty. This improvement has been due more to education than to any other single factor. Many Nevisians migrated to England, America and Canada, and to other Caribbean islands. Because of their high level of education, they prospered and sent money back to their families in Nevis. Remittance money litterally kept the island afloat in the mid-20th century.

Tourism has grown significantly in the last decade, but not to the point where it has overwhelmed local culture. Government has wisely required tourist facilities to be of top quality only, and has avoided the mass tourism which has spoiled so many other Caribbean Islands. Government is also encouraging the development of Nevis as a sophisticated offshore financial center, to create another source of income. Again, because of the high level of local education, these endeavors have met with success.

Looking at gentle Nevis today, it is difficult to imagine it as having once been the focal point of European imperial conflicts, the site of significant military engagements and immense wealth. Its past was often violent, tragic and brutal. Nevisians today can be proud that they have lifted the island out of the wreckage left after the collapse of the sugar economy, and are charting a course to future prosperity.

Uniform Corp Parade for the Tenth Anniversary of Independence.

A VISITOR'S HANDBOOK

By Deborah Lellouch

Only a few days suffice to convince the visitor to Nevis that he has found a place of unique beauty and charm, a place which grows on you with each new discovery. The original Carib inhabitants called it "Oualie", or Land of Beautiful Water. The native pronunciation of Nevis is "Nee-vis", while St.Kitts is known locally as "Sinkits".

The beach at Hurricane Hill.

First, there is an intimacy with nature which appeals to all the senses: the gentle warmth of the sun; the cool breath of tradewinds; the soothing turquoise sea, ever near; the endless horizon; the riotous colors of bougainvillea with its red and purple and orange bracts, the flaming Royal Poinciana; the sounds of birds and bees and chirping things; the pandemonium of farmyard animals at daybreak; the unsolaced solo of the whip-poor-will at nightfall; the juicy sweetness of a freshly-picked mango; the silky smooth texture of a jelly coconut.

Then, there is the welcome, Nevis-style, with smiles and quiet hospitality that make you feel you are an invited guest to this island: You, here, now. It is the people who make the difference. There has always been a kinship, however polite and proper, between Nevisians and visitors. The experience is one of coming home to traditional values, even a tinge old-fashioned, often lost in the business of getting ahead in an urban society. Dress is informal, so there are few obvious distinctions between haves and have-nots. It is relaxing to be totally acceptable everywhere, as one is, and to leave one's hang-ups behind.

Welcome to a country where there is virtually no crime, where police are not armed – except for certain coastal patrols – and are generally more helpful than coercive. However, parking tickets at $25 E.C. do exist; so mind the curb markings! This is a society determined to remain drug free, with harsh sanctions of up to $100,000 E.C. and 5 years imprisonment for those who dare to flirt with the law. Death by hanging is still on the books. Even petty theft is extremely rare. The author once left her suitcase on the pier for several hours while she enjoyed a leisurely dinner, and returned to find it carefully guarded by the dockside regulars. A sense of security and confidence reigns.

Welcome to a country with the highest literacy rate in the Western Hemisphere: 98% of Nevisians read and write proficiently. Poetry and the Classics are frequently recited, debating teams compete in regional contests, and writing ability is encouraged from earliest grammar school. The British school system affords students a rigorous program which prepares them for advanced studies – usually at the University of the West Indies, the University of the Virgin Islands or in the United States or Britain. For those who enter the workworld, the level is roughly equivalent to completion of junior college.

Welcome to a health-conscious society where heart disease is rare, and smoking is almost non-existent, even in bars and restaurants. The chief medical officer at the hospital confirmed that eating disorders and the "pathologies of affluence" were largely absent in the local population. Cleanliness is a habit of daily life, and great attention is given to a neat appearance; witness the impeccably dressed and groomed school children, even at play. Sunday is an occasion to go "all out" in sartorial finery. Pristine white, from head to toe, is *de rigueur* in certain church communities.

In Nevis, the spontaneous is routine. How restrictive to adhere to a meticulous plan when one can "go with the flow", and allow the unexpected to happen. An elderly resident, once the town shoemaker, told me with no uncertain glee: "I surprised my mother at birth, as she was expecting a girl, and I have been surprising people ever since!" Disconcerting at first, this penchant for the "happening" becomes a source of anticipation and delight. This is not to say that serious matters do not receive timely attention: Bank and store hours, business appointments, transportation schedules and taxi drivers may be relied upon for exactitude.

What might be considered a humdrum occupation elsewhere, takes on a sense of purpose and importance in this well-integrated and harmonious society. Each profession, each endeavor, is worthy of respect as a "job well done". Sloppiness and shoddiness are simply not tolerated, and squandering of precious resources is severely reprimanded. Society sets a standard which each member is expected to meet. Goodness and excellence are the just measure of one's worth.

Social interaction has its rules in Nevis. When a point is to be made or a favor asked, one begins by inquiring about the other's health, family or business. Here a word of caution is appropriate: Almost all Nevisians are related in some way, and the person you are talking to is very likely the cousin of the person you are talking about. Besides, there is a sense of caring and responsibility towards one's physical neighbors, one's clients – a first loyalty which may mean that everyone cannot be accommodated at once. The corollary of this social cohesion is that gossip and rumors circulate at the speed of light, kindled by natural inquisitiveness and concern.

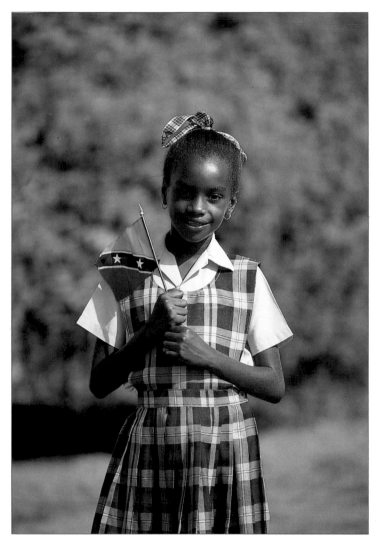

A student from the Charlestown prep school.

Nevisians share a proud awareness of the remarkable landscape features of their island, as seen from the air, the sea and the land, and a deep respect for the "genius of the place" (Alexander Pope, Essays on Man, 1733). Caring for the environment is very much an individual concern, contributing to a high level of public consciousness about the preservation and development of the natural resources of Nevis. Close cooperation beween non-profit organizations and the government is a guarantee of success. The Caribbean Conservation Association, with technical assistance from the Island Resources Foundation, has embarked on an ambitious program to strengthen environmental non-governmental organizations (NGO's), based on the belief that institutional partnerships between the private and public sector will promote ecologically sound development in the region.

The Nevis Historical and Conservation Society, founded in 1980, has led the effort to preserve the natural culture and historical heritage of the island. In 1988, with support from the World Wildlife Fund, the group began monitoring fragile and threatened areas that include coastal lands, wetlands, and uplands. NHCS also operates the Alexander Hamilton Museum and the Nelson Museum at Morning Star; acts as a "national trust", maintaining the archives and library of Nevis history; carries out research and assesses the environmental impact of development; and publishes a widely-read newsletter.

The Nevis Environmental Education Committee, recipient of the 1990 Eastern Caribbean "Earth Day" award, sponsors a wide variety of programs: campaigns in favor of endangered species such as the brown pelican (national bird) and the sea turtle; beach clean-ups and waste inventory; village improvement competitions; radio talk shows; and children's summer activities.

When it comes to Ecotourism, Nevis prones the philosophy that a healthy environment generates a healthy tourism market. As you become better acquainted with Nevis and its people, and perhaps begin to identify with their values, it is almost certain that you, too, will become protective of this place; that you will want to preserve your discovery so that it remains a "treasure" for generations to come.

TRADITIONS AND CUSTOMS

By Deborah Lellouch

Two very special festivities rhythm the Nevisian calendar: Culturama (from the last Thursday in July to the first Monday in August) and Carnival Celebrations (from Christmas Eve to the day after New Year's). A third holiday took on exceptional significance in 1993, as the Federation of St. Kitts and Nevis celebrated its Tenth Anniversary of Independence on September 19th.

CULTURAMA is a time of homecoming for expatriate Nevisians, wherever they may be for reasons of education, profession or family. Guests from abroad are also invited to share in this festive portrayal of traditional life in Nevis. Activities are so numerous and engaging that it takes considerable stamina to survive the entire fortnight ! 'Round-the-clock festivities culminate in a seafaring party on J'ouvert Morning when revelers "jam" until they drop.

In 1974, members of the Nevis Drama and Cultural Society, along with other enlightened citizens, set out to preserve and revive traditional folklore, arts and crafts, and musical talent. During the first decade, funds were raised to build a cultural center at Grove Park where theatrical productions and concerts are now held. Local artists display paintings, pottery, handmade linens, basketry and woodwork throughout Charlestown. Colorful booths materialize overnight at the waterfront, and serve up a movable feast of local specialities: barbecued chicken and ribs, seafood, rotis, patés, corn on the cob, and homemade pies and cakes.

Every evening, crowds flock to the open-air theater to attend the Youth Talent Show, the Beauty Pageant (including a much-ballyhooed bathing suit contest), and the Calypso Competition. Musical entries are aired on the radio for weeks, and excitement builds up to the final night when contestants rival one another with elaborate costumes and staging for the title of "Calypso Monarch". Strutting roosters, bridal parties in drag and other preposterous antics keep the audience rocking with laughter and applause. The winner is assured of the Number One spot on the Nevis Hit Parade and throughout the Leeward Islands.

Miss Culturama.

CARNIVAL, or CHRISTMAS SPORTS, derives its sources from ancient African rituals brought to Nevis by plantation workers centuries ago. Prior to Emancipation, Christmas Sports provided an outlet for traditional narratives, dancing, music, food and religious practices which were suppressed by the prevailing European culture. The players evolved a rich oral tradition, and succeeded admirably in exposing – through myriad disguises and impersonations – the gross injustice, social hypocrisy and moral deficiencies of the upper-class plantocracy. Today, the Sports are not only an expression of this heritage, but a living repository which has grown to include such diverse influences as the American Western and Tarzan of the Apes. Despite their outwardly fanciful and outrageous form, these proverbs and rhymes serve as an effective linguistic tool in provoking serious thought about obvious truths and familiar experiences.

The remembered delight of Christmases past is evident in these recollections of a Nevisian friend:

"You didn't have to see them to know they were coming! Troupes of masqueraders wearing trinkets and Christmas bells could be heard from afar, backed by the melodious sounds of a string or steel band and the driving beat of the big drum. Here and there, they would stop and have displays. Biblical stories, like David and Goliath, were classics. Slugging matches would break out, and the Sergeant would arrive to pacify and handcuff the belligerents. Clowns and Mummies and Bulls entertained the throngs crowding the streets."

Traditional parade costume.

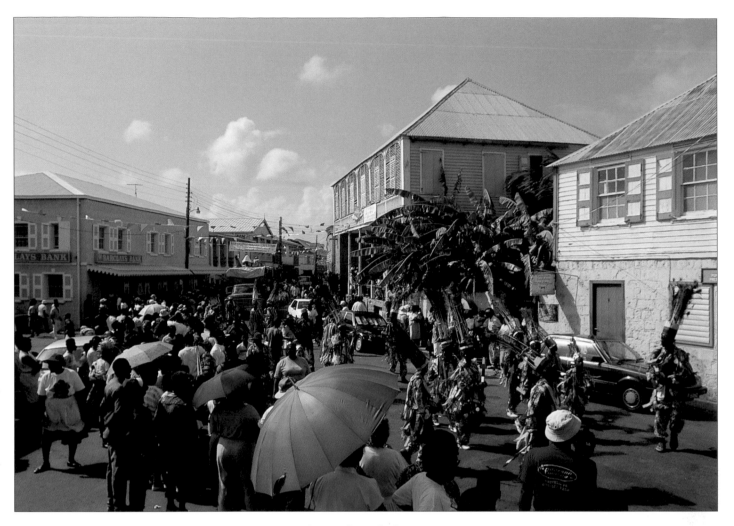

The parade in Charlestown.

"Most fantastic of all was the Sagwa Group, which picked up on real-life events during the year and mimicked them right in your own backyard: Neighborhood feuds, pillow-stuffed pregnant daughters trying to fool their mothers into believing they had done no wrong... Anyone was fair game for public ridicule. They brought suitcases of costumes. And when the music stopped, they would change around and commence a new scene. There were amazing stunts and acrobatics, and the rhythm really went to your head. It was hilarious!"

"Other troupes included the Carib Indians, fierce and vicious savages dressed very scantily, with wild-looking faces. They could not be controlled. Moving like they were crazed. Jumping on roofs. You never knew where they were coming from, nor when they would rush the crowd, sending terrified children running to their Momma's. No high heels when you came into town; shoes were worn for speed and agility. No one to save you, either. Just your luck. Policemen would stand back and laugh at your predicament."

"Cowboys would clatter into town on horseback, spinning pop guns and shooting from their holsters, while Indians in feathered headdress gave blood-curdling war whoops. They studied the Westerns at the local cinema and knew their moves to perfection."

Traditional dance troupes, beautifully dressed in floral prints and shimmering velvet, perform the Cake Walk and the French Quadrilles - just as they did in the old days for the pleasure of plantation owners and their guests. Museum groups are always researching documents to draw inspiration for their repertory.

Moko-jumbies, who originated hundreds of years ago in Guinea, West Africa, are being revived today in carnivals throughout the Caribbean. Towering twelve feet into the air on wooden stilts, defying the laws of balance as they dance and sway, they are thought to escape the gravitational forces of the earth. The analogy suggests that by doing these amazing feats, man has the ability to surpass the traps which life sets for him. Mocko-jumbies, literally "doctors of the spirit", are thought to protect people from evil in the New Year, and are loved and revered by young and old alike.

Yuletide fare features such festive foods as spit-roasted suckling pig, rice and peas, cassava bread, johnnycakes and blood pudding. Christmas-red sorrel is the typical tipple of the Season. Served fermented or unfermented, it is a rather bland drink until properly doctored up with spices and a generous dose of rum. This is indeed a perfect time to join in the fun and merrymaking: to partake in customs as rich as fruitcake; to revel in festivities as colorful as Carnival; to feel the warmth of the Christmas spirit without having to bundle up. In sum, to enjoy Nevisian hospitality at its holiday best.

Schools' Patriotic Program.

The twin-island Federation of St. Kitts-Nevis celebrated its Tenth Anniversary of Independence from Great Britain in a fanfare of official activities, and in sober reflection about the difficulties inherent in the governance of political autonomy. All in all, the tone was serious and introspective: How far have we come? What are the challenges of the next decade? How can we improve the relationship between our islands to achieve greater harmony of purpose? What is our role in regional and international politics? Many commemorative articles, poems and prayers reflected these concerns on the part of the citizenry.

The festivities, inaugurated by Premier Vance Amory, had a civic or cultural theme: Sports Competition for children born in 1983 in cricket, football and athletics; National Day of Prayer; Patriotic Youth Rally; Festival of Choirs; Senior Citizens' Day; and the Uniformed Parade. The week-long celebration was the occasion for a flurry of parties and receptions which honored government officials and visiting dignitaries. Many Nevisians crossed over to St. Kitts, and vice versa, so as not to miss the highlights of the program.

The Cultural Complex in Charlestown.

Five times a year – Easter Monday, Whit Monday, the first Sunday of August (Culturama), Independence Day and Boxing Day – the Nevis Turf & Jockey Club organizes races at the picturesque Indian Castle Raceway. This is an event not to be missed!
The track itself is unique: a simple dirt and grass loop, with occasional protruding stones, which wends precariously up and downhill against a backdrop of wildly-crashing waves on Nevis' southern coast.

The horses are just as rugged and untamed as the setting itself, bearing names such as "Me No 'Fraid", "Hold Tight", "Maritsa Killer", "Thunderhead" and "Ganja Man". One thing they are: ready and willing. Training often means swimming several miles in the ocean before taking a spin around the track. And they can flat-out run! Not necessarily in the right direction, however, as was the case at the Independence Day Race. In one heat, three out of five jockeys parted company with their mounts, as the horses unexpectedly cut back into the paddock *au passage*. Another race saw all but two horses eliminated for repeated false starts. Yet another event had spectators gasping as one of the horses raced around the track backwards, narrowly missing the thundering pack head-on. Jockeys and amateur riders enjoy easy camaraderie, and revel in the pride of their hard-won trophies. Guest horses and jockeys from nearby Antigua have the spectators hooting and stomping. Adrenaline is running high. Children are kept happy eating popsicles and sticky candy. Young men are showing off their savvy at the betting booth. And a wonderful afternoon is had by all !

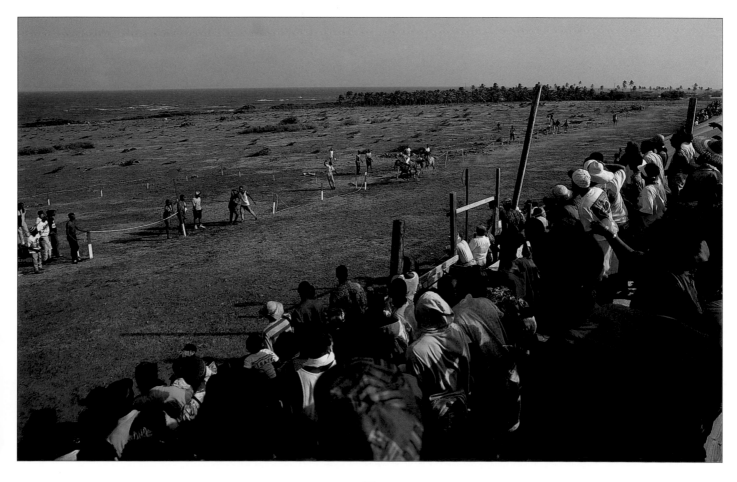

RELIGION

By Deborah Lellouch

Religion, in both content and structure, has always played a central role in the life of Nevis. The island is divided into five parishes: St. Thomas' Lowland; St. James' Windward; St. Paul's Charlestown; St. George's Gingerland; and St. John's Figtree. These Anglican churches were all founded in the Seventeenth Century by the English settlers. They were originally built of wood, and later rebuilt in local stone. Sephardic Jews and Quakers were also present in Nevis in the 1600's. In the early 1700's, Roman Catholics were banned by law from the island, and not fully rehabilitated until 1882.

Cornerstones, plaques and graveyards chronicle the lives of governors, bishops, missionaries and original Nevisian families, whose names are carried on today. St. Thomas', built in 1643, is thought to be one of the oldest churches in the Caribbean. St. James' Windward, first constructed in 1679, contains a rare crucifix with a black Christ. St. John's Figtree displays the marriage certificate of Lord Nelson, Britain's most famous admiral, on the occasion of his marriage to a Nevisian beauty, Fanny Nisbet, in 1787.

It was about this time that Methodist missionaries arrived in Nevis to evangelize both blacks and whites, and organized the first Sunday and Day School for children of slaves.

Fig Tree Anglican Church.

The suspected connection to abolitionist movements led to the bombing, in 1797, of a Methodist chapel where the missionary, John Brownell, was preaching. In true Christian spirit, charges were not pressed, and no further acts of violence were reported. In 1826, church records show 802, members, 601 of whom were slaves.

Today, the Anglican Church remains dominant, although Baptists, Seventh Day Adventists, Evangelical and Pentecostal sects have become very much a part of the religious scene. Whatever one's spiritual affiliation, Sunday is a time of church-going in Nevis.

The religious content of Nevisian life can be felt in every area of human endeavor. Thanks and praise are often rendered to the "Almighty" on public occasions. The National Anthem contains the exhortation: "With God in all our struggles." And one frequently hears, "God willing", or "God bless you", as a parting remark. Special prayers are offered for the many Nevisians who sail upon the seas. Church communities welcome the visitor and inquire about his well-being on the island. What was my surprise to meet an organist and choir director from my hometown in Virginia on an exchange visit to St. Paul's Church. It seemed the congregation sang with more fervor that Sunday morning.

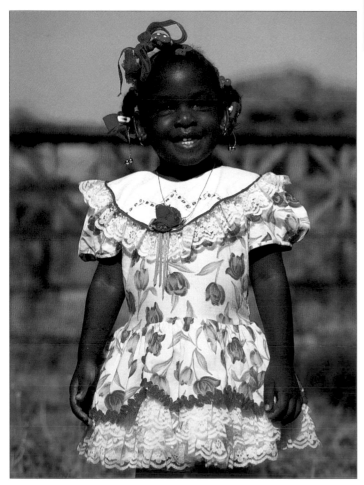

All dressed up for Sunday School.

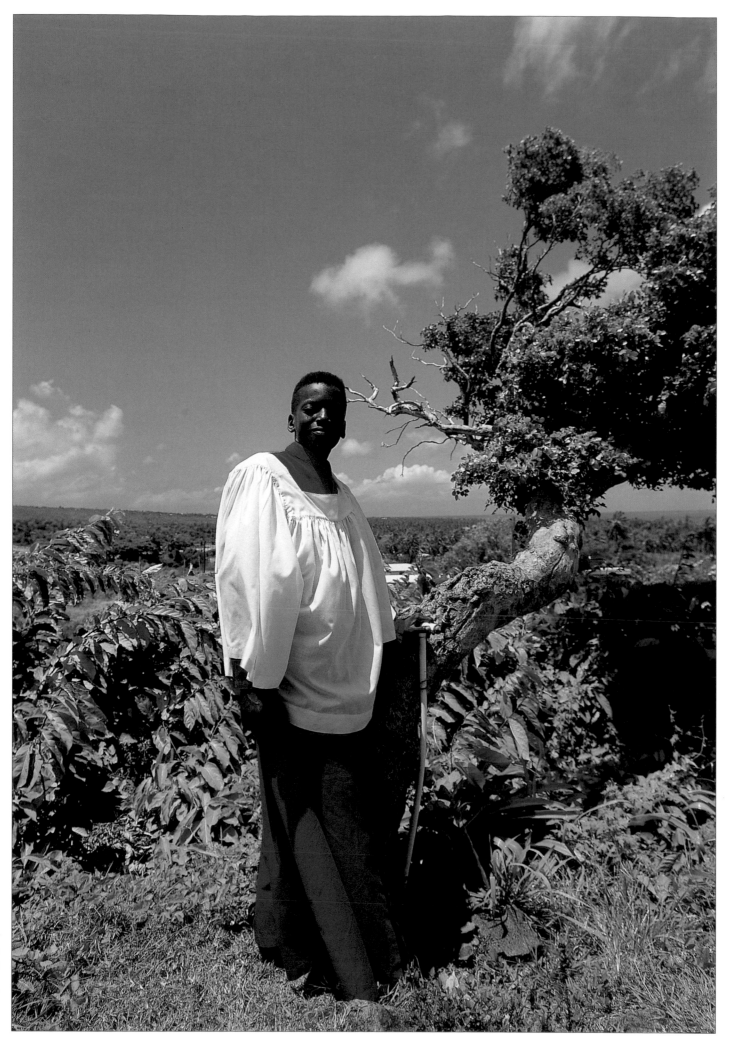

Choirboy at St. Paul's Anglican Church.

POLITICAL LIFE

By Deborah Lellouch

St. Kitts and Nevis is a sovereign democratic state within the British Commonwealth of nations. The two islands officially function as one, in a unique form of binary federation, which accords considerable autonomy to each government.

The political structure is based on the British system of parliamentary democracy, with separate unicameral legislatures consisting of fourteen members in St. Kitts, and nine members in Nevis having guaranteed representation in the federal administration. The statutory head of parliament is Queen Elizabeth II, represented in St. Kitts by a Governor General, who appoints the Prime Minister from the majority party in the House of Assembly. In like manner, the Deputy Governor of Nevis names the Premier, and, upon his advice, the Ministers of Government. The Nevis Cabinet is fully responsible for determining policy regarding the economic and social development of the island.

For nine years following Independence, the Nevis Reformation Party (NRP) held the reins of government, led by then-Premier Simeon Daniels, in alliance with the People's Action Movement (PAM) of St. Kitts. This coalition, known as the "eight-day wonder", averted Nevisian secession from the impending joint move to Independence — by a one-seat majority — over the Labor Party which had wielded power for thirty years without regard to the prerogatives of Nevis.

The Honorable Kennedy A.Simmonds, Prime Minister of St. Kitts and Nevis; and The Honorable Vance Amory, Premier of Nevis.

Following the elections of June 1, 1992, the Nevis Island Administration passed into the hands of the Concerned Citizens Movement (CCM), under the leadership of Premier Vance Amory. Ministerial tasks are largely shared by all members of the Cabinet. The Premier himself subsumes the responsibilities of Minister of Finance, Education, Health, Tourism, Trade, Industry, Development Planning, Youth, Women and Community Affairs. This is a "pitch-in" style of management, by any standards. While it is true that problems should be more manageable in a small independent nation, delegating authority is made difficult by the fact that there is only a handful of top-level administrators, and the demands are overwhelming.

Nevis is the kind of place where any concerned citizen can have the Premier's ear to present a problem or suggest a solution to an existing one. Fortunately, there is no dearth of ingenuity and know-how here. Nor is there any lack of good-will on the part of its citizens; examples of fruitful cooperation abound. One can feel confident that Nevis will meet the challenges of the next decade with characteristic resolve and determination to succeed. In the Premier's words:
"May the future be bright for us in all aspects of our endeavours."

THE ECONOMY

By Deborah Lellouch

In determining the wealth of a nation, statisticians often consider only economic indicators. The people of Nevis have other criteria in mind as they look toward future development. First among these, is the preservation and enhancement of the quality of life.

Although the tourism sector and related construction and service activities (transport, banking, realty, etc...) are projected to reach high levels over the next five years, considerable attention is being given to the various consequences of this development, while at the same time taking special care not to neglect other areas of economic growth, such as agriculture and manufacturing. The traditional dependency on sugar production, which has steadily declined over the years to its current level of 6% of GDP, has been replaced by a growing number of small industries which produce electronic equipment, women's apparel, plastic utensils, electrical appliances (assembly and packaging), beer, soft drinks and furniture. According to statistics compiled by the USDC, the electronics industry in St. Kitts and Nevis is one of the largest producers of transformers, transducers and other electronic components, per capita, in the world.

Raw materials for use in manufacturing available locally include kaolin clay deposits and activated carbon. The island's abundant water supply gives producers an invaluable advantage in a part of the world where scarcity is the norm. The Prospect Industrial Estate in Nevis, owned, serviced and managed by the St. Kitts and Nevis Development Bank, consists of fourteen acres and is located on the outskirts of Charlestown. A new power plant has also been built at the Estate. On-site factory shells are available on a lease or lease-purchase basis. Alternatively, investors may construct their own factory.

Economic growth in St. Kitts and Nevis, in real terms, has averaged 5% since the beginning of the 1980's. Under the leadership of a stable, dynamic and cooperative democratic government, increased private sector investment has been given the highest priority and support. To encourage new business ventures, a broad-based selection of fiscal incentives and concessions has been introduced:

- Duty-free imports for use in manufacturing and hotel resort accommodations;

- Tax holidays ranging from ten to fifteen years, depending on the amount of value added to the product locally;

- Training programs for local employees, funded jointly by the Organization of American States (OAS) and the U.S. Agency for International Development (USAID);

- Banking amenities, including the operation of foreign currency accounts;

- Repatriation of profits.

- There is no personal income tax in St. Kitts and Nevis.

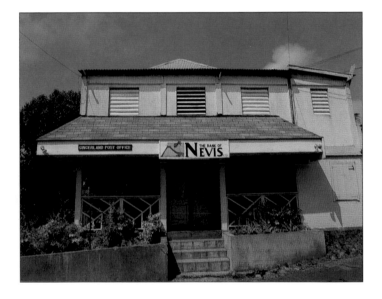

Companies are provided with a further tax concession at the end of the tax holiday period: It is, in effect, a rebate of a portion of income tax paid based on export profits as a percentage of total profits. Many additional trade incentives are provided through the Caribbean Common Market (CARICOM), the Caribbean Basin Initiative (CBI), the Business Advisory Services (BAS), the Lomé Convention, which gives privileged access to EEC countries, and the Overseas Private Investment Corporation (OPIC), a self-sustaining U.S. Government Agency, which provides a variety of services to encourage private sector investment in developing countries. Preferential U.S. Tariff Schedules (Items 806 and 807), provide additional relief to processing plants based in St. Kitts and Nevis. U.S. Internal Revenue Code Section 936, by providing special credit for certain income of qualifying corporations in Puerto Rico and the U.S. Virgin Islands, has created funds of approximately $7 billion to finance twin plant development or production-sharing ventures with CBI beneficiaries.

St. Kitts and Nevis have a combined labor force of approximately 22,000, which is adaptable, trainable and possesses a high degree of manual dexterity. Once again, it is the people who make the qualitative difference.

The advanced telecommunications network operated by SKANTEL (St. Kitts and Nevis Telecommunications, Ltd.) is fully digital and includes direct dialing to worldwide destinations, telex and fax services.

Two major development projects will further enhance the present transportation and cargo facilities of Nevis: the extension of the runway at Newcastle Airport to accommodate larger aircraft; and the modernisation of the Port of Charlestown, scheduled for 1995-96. A major road resurfacing project is also under way.

THE "GRASS ROOTS" ECONOMY

If you should happen to take the St. Kitts-Nevis ferry, "Caribe Queen", you will observe a burst of activity as you arrive at the Charlestown dock: people meeting people; people picking up packages; people dropping off packages; people inquiring whether they received any packages; people exchanging money for packages, and vice versa; taxis picking up people with packages. It never seems to stop, the coming and going. Your simple conclusion is that the ferry provides a vital link between the Sister Islands. And you are right!

Life in Nevis, for most people, is punctuated by these frequent hops to surrounding islands. Chances are, their mother, brother, aunt or cousin lives in St. Kitts, or maybe in St. Martin. Children go to spend the summer with their grandma, and return laden with toys and gifts. Family reunions – a big thing throughout the Caribbean – bring long-lost relatives together. Besides the obvious social aspect, these family ties are often the basis for some sort of commerce.

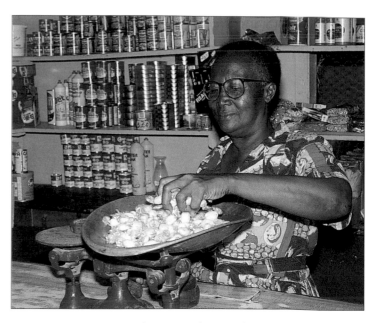

A shop on Hanley's Road.

The importance of the off-island economy cannot be overemphasized. The very nature and specificity of a small island engenders the need to trade. There is the access to a larger market: Fruits and vegetables growing in abundance in Nevis, furniture and other handcrafted objects find their way to willing customers on other islands. Much-needed products can be made available locally. Besides the usual foods and supplies, clothing and domestic goods, there is a lively commerce in tools, auto parts, vehicles, appliances and building materials. This, in turn, sustains maritime shipping and its ancillary corps of stevedores, customs agents, dock workers and crew. The cargo trade, among man's most ancient economic activities, is not only thriving today, but is assured of tremendous development in the future. Another important aspect of the off-island economy is the funneling of funds back into Nevis from expatriates whose trade or professional competence has led them to settle elsewhere – in the Caribbean, or in the United States and Canada, where large communities of Nevisians can be found.

With the demise of the large sugar plantations, the economic pattern of land use has progressively changed. Agricultural activity on Nevis has become the domain of less than a thousand full-time farmers, who produce a range of crops such as yams, peanuts, carrots, cabbage, eggplants, cucumbers, tomatoes, peppers, pumpkins, peas and beans. They are aided by government programs which provide irrigation systems, tractors and harvesting equipment. What does not end up in Nevisian kitchens, is sent over to St. Kitts. Some sea island cotton is still grown and sold exclusively to Japan. Copra was once produced on coconut plantations and exported to Dominica; however this activity was severely curtailed by Hurricane Hugo in 1989. Bamboo and climbing palms are being utilized in the production of bamboo and rattan furniture. The Nevis Beekeeper's Cooperative was organized in 1987, by a volunteer from the British Voluntary Service Overseas, and now numbers over 70 bee hives.

From the large animal population used to work the sugar estates, livestock owners have turned to the production of domestic meats and by-products. There are currently only five large estates where grazing lands are available: two are government-owned and three are private. Poultry is raised throughout the island and is readily available in the markets. A modern abattoir, with complete cold-storage facilities, processes the livestock for consumption. Many families keep small herds of goats and sheep for domestic use. Pigs and chickens are also raised in the backyard. Donkeys are still the preferred carriers for transporting fodder or produce from the hillsides or ghauts into town. Fishing activity is still very productive in the waters surrounding Nevis. Fishermen and lobstermen set traps, or "pots", three or four miles offshore, which they check on a regular basis, or employ nets, spears or trawling methods. Small wooden boats with outboard motors are built locally at Gallows Bay, and can be seen plying their way along the coast. The Nevis Fishing Cooperative provides cleaning and cold storage facilities.

Donkey - powered cart.

A FISH STORY

One Saturday morning about 10:00 A.M., the author and photographer could be observed waiting expectantly on the beach at Indian Castle, scanning the horizon for the tiny dot of a fishing boat returning with its catch. Brooker and Teddy and the others had set out before dawn with the hope of bringing in a bumper crop of lobsters. It has something to do with the full moon and the tides and the sex life of crustaceans.

We were not disappointed! Shimmering and slithering fish in the morning sun, and lobsters cringing furtively under the prow, made for an awesome catch. The dazzling array of colors led me to fancy that the Creator had dipped into the rainbow's palette to paint these beautiful swimmers: Red and yellow-tailed snappers, hinds, wrenchmen, wahoos and the technicolor toms, in vivid and exotic hues. The variety of shapes and markings was astounding. We couldn't resist the temptation to pick them up and admire their features. "Watch out for the Old Wife's gaping jaw!" we were warned: "She is vicious... but delicious."

Everyone gave a hand to haul the heavy boat onto the beach. Repeated "Heave-ho's" were necessary. Many smiles and photos later, the happy crew packed the miraculous catch into waiting ice chests, and drove off to the market just in time for the throngs of Saturday shoppers.

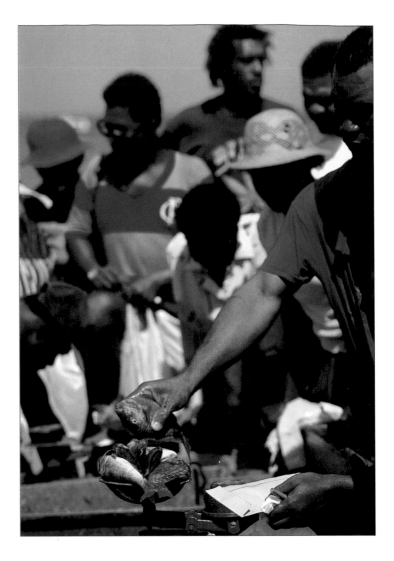

Fish market at Charlestown, on Gallows Bay.

The colorful catch.

TOURISM

Nevisian officials are very proud of the high standards of their hotels and tourist facilities. They are doing their utmost to preserve and further promote these national assets. The Tourism Office, located on Main Street in downtown Charlestown, can give visitors all kinds of practical information about hotels and activities on the island, including maps.
Be they hotel managers or simply passersby, Nevisians will always go out of their way to make visitors feel welcome, and their stay as enjoyable as possible.
From the pages of its very rich history, the island maintains many historical landmarks. Visiting the ruins of old plantations, browsing through museums, and studying the architecture of traditional buildings is a sure way to make exciting and rewarding discoveries.
What makes the island so special, is a rare and delicate blend of culture and gentility, in an exceptionally beautiful natural setting.

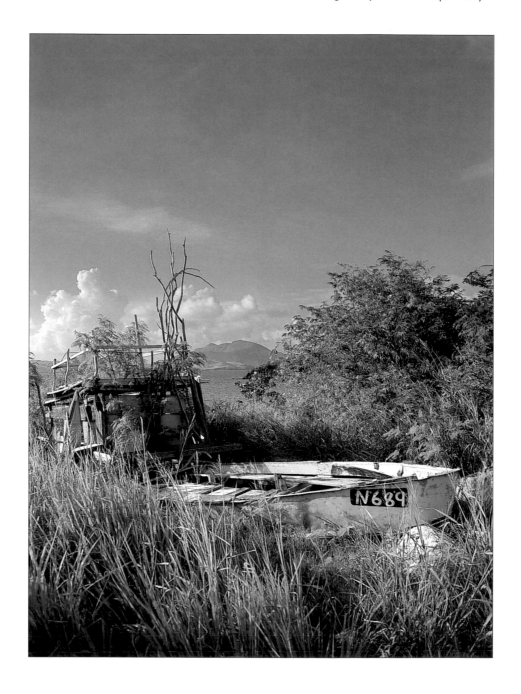

Throughout the year, the life of the inhabitants is marked by colorful and festive events. Visitors are kindly invited to join in and celebrate! The whole island dances to the rhythm of Calypso music, and there is a magic atmosphere reflected in the bright costumes and happy faces of the population.

Nevis uniquely combines all the ingredients for the best vacation of your life. It is the ideal place for newlyweds on their honeymoon, for active families, or for those who just want to relax and get away from it all. Nevis is indeed a paradise, to which visitors return again and again. Many have built vacation homes, or have even settled there for a lifetime.

A Nevisian Beauty.

The Indians who lived on the island when Christopher Columbus arrived, did not survive the successive waves of colonization, and quickly died out, either because they contracted diseases brought in from Europe, or because of ill-treatment on the part of the invaders.

Throughout its history, Nevis has been settled by peoples of many nationalities and religions: After the Indians came the Spaniards, the British, the French, the Dutch – of Catholic, Protestant or Jewish descent – as well as a variety of adventure-seekers, who had fled for political reasons, or who came to bury a shady past and make a fortune from the sugar cane culture.

Because of the extensive development of agriculture in the Caribbean, especially sugar cane, the African slave trade flourished from 1500 to 1860.This multiracial society had a rigid hierarchy, from the large plantation owners who wielded political and economic might, to the slaves who lived in unbearable poverty.

At the zenith of sugar production in Nevis, 10,000 of the island's 23,000 acres were devoted to cane. To meet the strong demand for farm labor, many black slaves were brought to the island. They rapidly outnumbered the European plantation owners. Only through terror was the minority plantocracy able to keep the upper hand, ruthlessly crushing the slaves' attempts at rebellion. However, after centuries of suffering, their descendants can at last see justice being rendered.

Although land remained in the hands of the planter class following Emancipations in 1838, the collapse of the world market signaled the demise of the large estates. By the time the last sugar mill was shut down in 1958, much of the land had been divided into smaller parcels for homesites and for agricultural use by former sharecroppers. Today, 80% of the homeowners in Nevis hold title to their lot. Since Independence, Nevisians have developed sound policies in the management of their natural and cultural heritage, thus restoring their island to a modern-day semblance of paradise lost.

The present population figure stands at 9,300 inhabitants, not counting native Nevisians living abroad, which would increase this figure two-fold.

Thanks to better standards of living and hygiene, the infant mortality rate on the island has significantly decreased in the past decades. The population is very young, and there are many beautiful and healthy children to symbolize the happiness and rejuvenation of the Nevisian people.

Apart from the native population, there is a small community of expatriate Americans and Europeans, who live in Nevis on a temporary or permanent basis: Some stay and work for only a few years; others choose to settle there for the rest of their lives; and some are the descendants of the original colonizers. But the bond among all these people is a common love for this, their island.

"The Queen" at Jessups' Village.

Don and Carol Peterson have spent more than fifteen years on the island.
They have a passion for plants, and especially Hibiscus. Their company, "Absolutely Bushed", manages projects from landscaping to interior decorating.
Carol spends the morning caring for her "babies", and always picks the freshest blooms to decorate the table.

This shoemaker, has a tiny shop on the righthand side of the main road, past the Eva Wilkin Gallery, on the way to Golden Rock Estate.
It is made of wooden planks and corrugated metal, just big enough to contain all the shoes he is repairing.

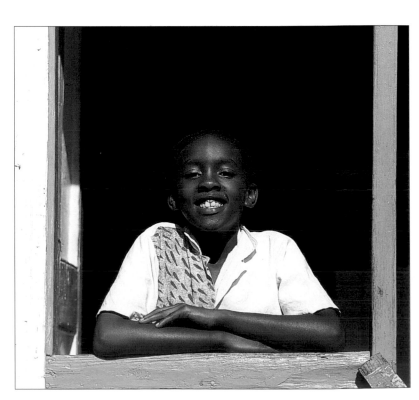

A young girl who lives in Butlers' Village in a wonderful house painted to match the Nevis sky.

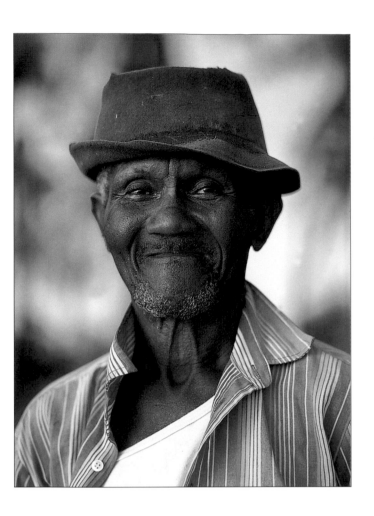

Mr. Martin was a fisherman, who became a Christian after a miraculous survival. Every evening, he goes to the beach for a swim, and to admire the beauty of the sunset at Jessups Bay.

Chantal Paris is a representative of charm, from the Model Agency of Nevis.

This fisherman catches his dinner with a gossamer net att sundown on Pinney's beach.

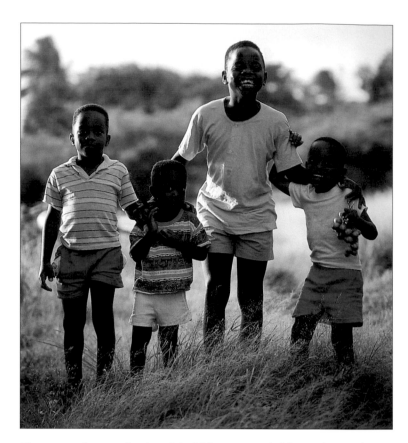

Vincent Hubbard is the President of the Nevis Historical and Conservation Society, and an archaeologist from the team which excavated the Jewish Synagogue in Charlestown, and many other sites. He is also the Managing Director of Morning Star Holdings, and an expert in offshore corporate formation.

This juicy fruit is the local bubble gum. Children always know where to find a genip tree growing.

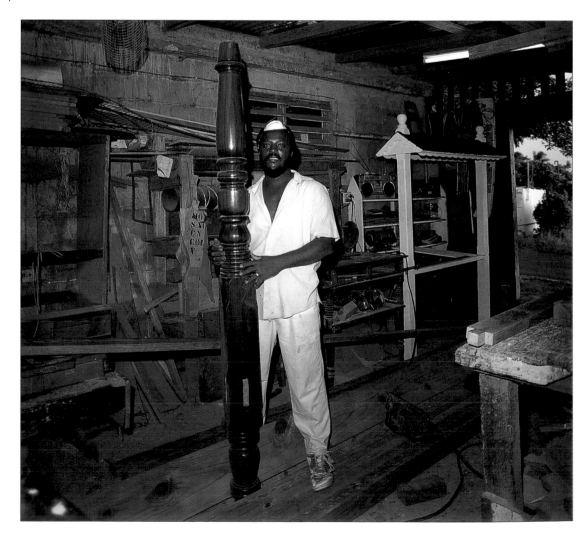

Woodcraft is an important activity on the island.
A Nevisian cabinet-maker displays a finely-sculpted bedpost.

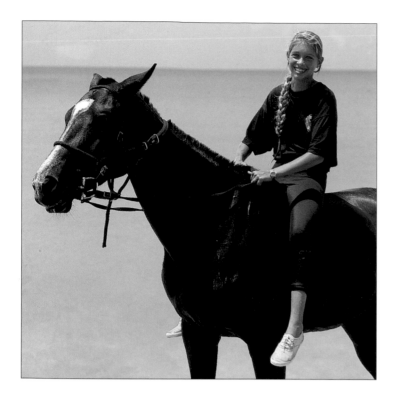

Nothing is more relaxing, for horse and rider alike, than a cantor along the water's edge.
Is this Katie, or her identical twin sister, Chrissie?
Both are excellent riders who have won amateur races at Indian Castle.

Oral Daniel is a native of Nevis who emigrated to Germany where he was an Entertainer and producer of musical events. He has come back home for his family, and to develop cultural activities on the island.

Quentin Henderson was sent in 1987 by Voluntary Service Overseas, the British peace corps, to develop beekeeping as a small industry on the island. The earliest reference to bees in Nevis dates from 1716. For many years, people known as "honey cutters" collected the honey from wild nests as a marginal activity.
Today, the production of honey and beeswax candles is a fast-growing industry.

ARCHITECTURE

The climate and history of the Caribbean have developed an indigenous lifestyle, which, in turn, has an obvious influence on the architecture. For instance, most houses have a veranda and a natural ventilation system generated by air drafts. Louvered windows let the air in and out, cooling down the house. The roof framework is raised high, to attract the air upwards.

Basic construction materials were, and still are, a dark volcanic stone, and wood. Wooden buildings are lighter in structure and more fragile. Stone structures, being assembled with a coral powder cement, are sturdier and can better resist earthquakes. The usual building technique involves a combination of both materials. The ground floor is typically made of stone while the second story is wooden. This provides for greater comfort and security regardless of climatic conditions.

Coconut shingles.

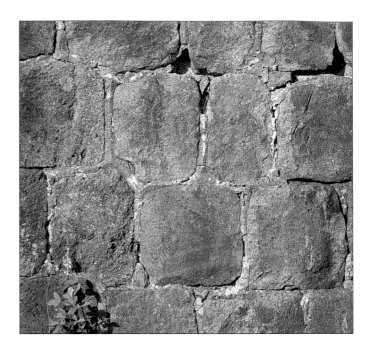

Volcanic stone.

The Sand Box Tree in Charlestown.

44

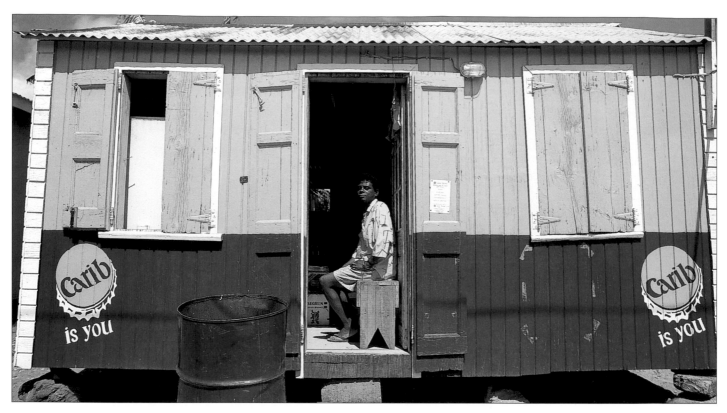

A bar in Charlestown painted in the colors of Carib Beer.

One of Charlestown's characteristic features comes from the fact that, for centuries, maritime activity has been the basis of the economy. The main buildings all look out to the sea, and streets are parallel to the beach to make it easier for ships to unload freight. This typical pattern helps visitors understand what life was like in the past on this island, once among the most prosperous in the Caribbean.

The brightly-painted houses along the roads add a cheerful note to the landscape. They are raised off the ground on stone or brick blocks to let the water flow underneath. Another reason for this system is that houses must be transportable, as people do not necessarily own the land under their house.

Chapel Street facing the ocean.   *Typical Nevisian house.*

New River Estate.

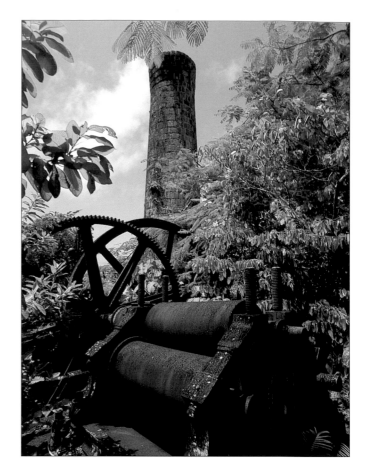

Old Manor Estate.

The Plantation Inns are wonderful vestiges for amateurs of history and architecture. Thanks to the careful maintenance and restoration work undertaken by their owners, it is now possible to go back in time, and imagine what life was like in the days of the sugar estates. At some plantations such as New River Estate, Old Manor or Golden Rock, it is possible to visualize the sugar processing facilities in their heyday. Windmills are also part of the landscape. Their conic shape used to be a familiar sight all over the island. During the golden age of sugar production, it is said that there were up to 200 of them. Some were destroyed or are in ruins, but others have been restored and turned into elegant homes.

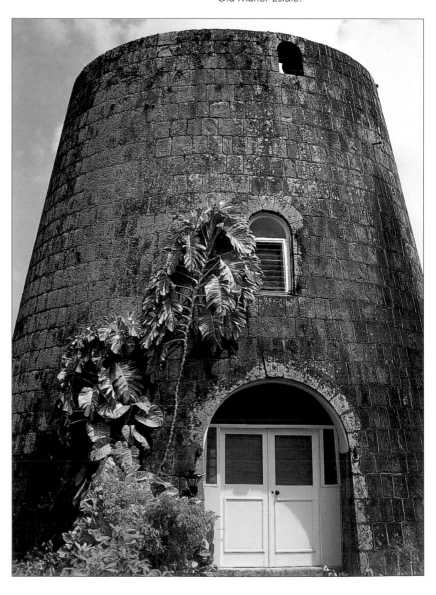

A well-restored mill at Golden Rock Estate.

Churches are also typical of the island. There are several types of structures, some of wood, others of stone, or even cement. The oldest are the Anglican stone churches, built by the British settlers starting in the mid-17th century. They have remarkably withstood the wear and tear of time. St. Thomas' church dates back to 1643. To this day, they are used as shelters during hurricanes.

The roofs of buildings are usually very wide because they are used to catch rainwater, which is filtered and stored in cisterns, before being boiled for domestic use.

St. Thomas' Anglican Church.

Regardless of the size of their house, Nevisians attach great importance to the exterior appearance, and especially to their gardens which usually abound with decorative flowers and plants. The rich volcanic soil of the island sustains a very luxuriant and diversified flora. Some amateur horticulturists have successfully started hibiscus, orchid and palm tree cultures.

The veranda is always the place where nature meets architecture.

A modern house in the spirit of the Caribbean to the south of the island.

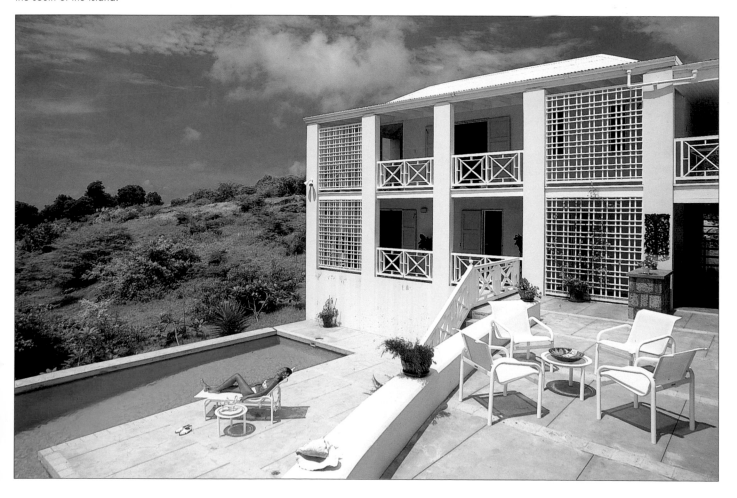

CHARLESTOWN

By Daphne L.Degazon Hobson   Architect and Historic Preservationist.

The chief town of the island, Charlestown, nestles along the eastern shore of an open bay or roadstead. With a present population of some 1,300 persons, it is the commercial, financial and administrative capital of the island having international and indigenous banks, modern telecommunications and car parking problems.

The narrow Main Street threads north-south through the historic towncenter on a meandering course. Small, two-story buildings of local stone and wood – many of which date from the early 19th century – line the street and create the sturdy and picturesque character of the town. Modern concrete homes and business places are springing up on the outskirts and hills above the historic core.

At two places Main Street opens into a square. The larger one, "Courthouse Square" or "Memorial Square", is dominated by the stately Courthouse built circa 1815. The D.R. Walwyn Square was recently named after a local son who, in the 1950's, opened the first indigenous bank, the Nevis Cooperative Banking Co. Ltd, located on Chapel Street.

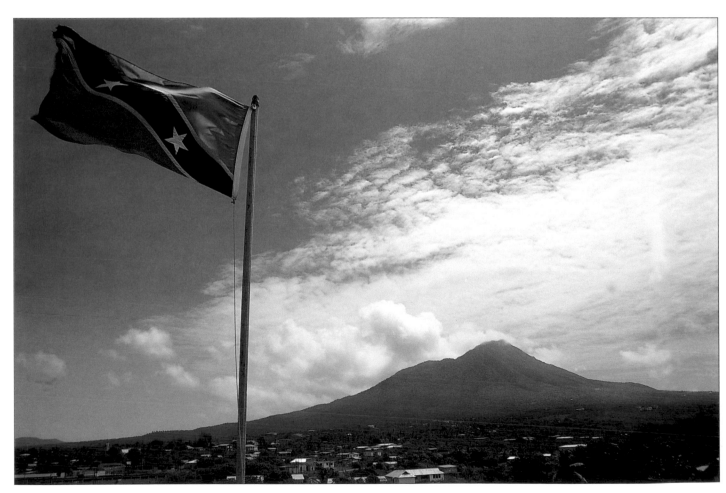

View from the Police station in the Bath House.

48

The pier.

In the center of the town, the "Treasury" (circa 1837) overlooks the Charlestown Pier which bustles with boats discharging food and building supplies, and the passengers of the "Caribe Queen", the St.Kitts to Nevis ferry.

In recent years, the Nevis Island Administration has been reclaiming land on the waterfront to protect the town from the rising sea-level and storm waves. But, until the 1950's, whilst "Sugar was King", the entire length of the Charlestown waterfront was a hive of activity. There were the lighters unloading estate supplies from ships riding at anchor in the roadstead. Ashore, small vessels, beached on the sand, were being packed with hogsheads of muscovados sugar from the "stanchions" (town stores) of the sugar estates.

The layout of old Charlestown's merchant houses along Main Street can still be discerned at Hamilton House, Barclays Bank and Long Stone House. Merchant houses on the waterfront had a massive seawall with a single gateway through which the supplies were hauled into a walled yard, and the barrels were rolled to the lighters. The sea walls at Hamilton House originally served to defend the town pier from attack from the sea as well as from wave action. For the merchant houses away from the waterfront, alleys running up from the beach provided access to shipping.

Barclays Bank.

Treasury Building.

The town was not formally planned or laid out. Charlestown grew from a coastal settlement known as the "Red Store House" until it was renamed for the restored monarch, Charles II, (circa 1671). The town and port grew on the area of solid land around the roadstead which could be adequately protected from enemy attack by the cross-fire from Forts Charles and Black Rocks (near St. Paul's Church).

In 1700, the population of Charlestown, of about 300, was polyglot: political and religious exiles, aristocrats, rebels, tradesmen and Sephardim. The Jews had introduced sugar cane plants and technology from Pernambuco, Brazil, to the Caribbean; they made up 25% of the town's population and were active in both plantation and commercial life until the mid -1700's, when they migrated to greener pastures.

The Jewish community is attested to by the "Jews Walk" and their well-kept cemetery on the outskirts of the historic town, with tombstones dating from the 18th century. An archaeological team is investigating a site for the remains of the synagogue mentioned in the Amsterdam Archives of the late 17th century.

During the early part of the 18th century, the assembly attempted to reduce the fire hazard in towns by ordering the destruction of thatched houses. By the middle of the century, there were a number of two-story stone buidings of impressive appearance with red tiled roofs. The birthplace of Alexander Hamilton, who framed the Constitution of the United States of America, was so described by the Methodist missionary, Thomas Coke, in 1787.

The Jewish Cemetery.

Alexander Hamilton's Birthplace.

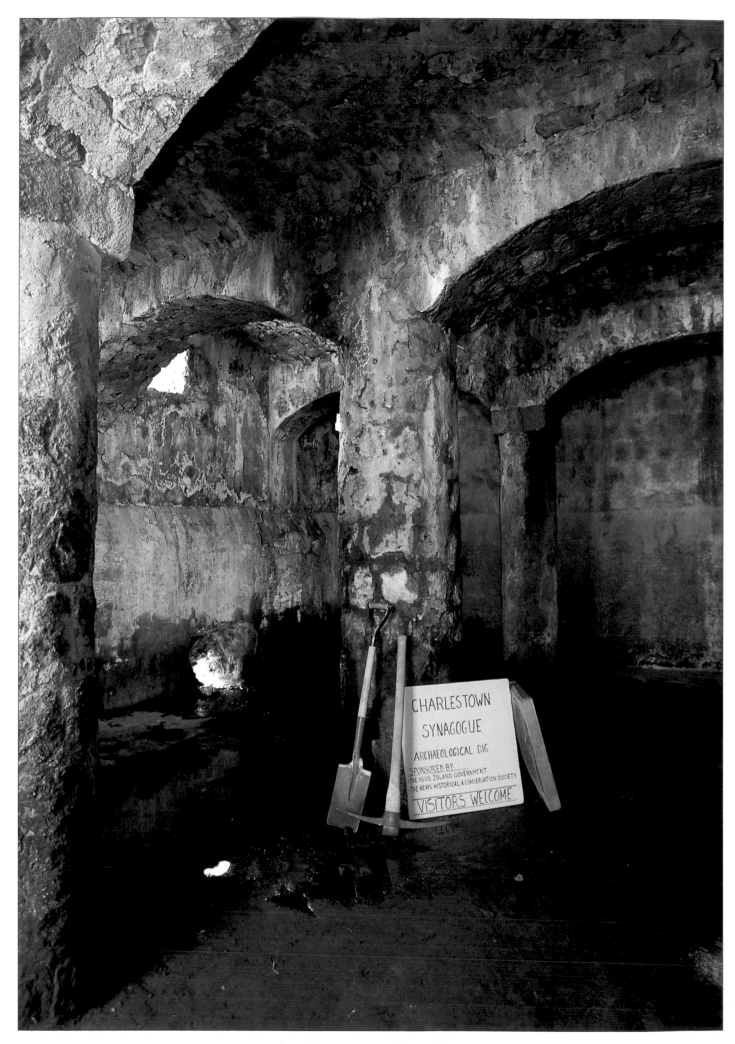

CHARLESTOWN
SYNAGOGUE
ARCHAEOLOGICAL DIG
SPONSORED BY
·THE NEVIS ISLAND GOVERNMENT
·THE NEVIS HISTORICAL & CONSERVATION SOCIETY
VISITORS WELCOME

The Oldest Synagogue in the Caribbean.

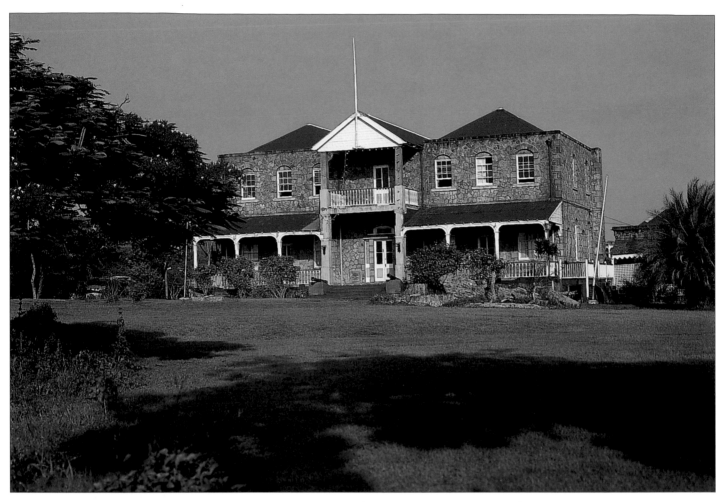

Courthouse.

Many of the 18th century stone houses collapsed during a series of disastrous earthquakes. This led to the practice of erecting an upper floor in wood over a stone ground floor. The tradition lasted into the 1950's, at which time the use of concrete blockwork was introduced for construction of the Charlestown Secondary School.

Successive generations of Nevisians, however, succeeded in erecting and maintaining their most important and sacred buildings of two-storys in the abundant local stone: the Long Stone House (circa 1800), the Bath Hotel (circa 1804), the Courthouse (circa 1815), Government House (circa 1909) and the churches.

Government House.

The Methodist Church on Chapel Street is a monument to the capabilities and determination of the newly-freed slaves who funded and constructed it in 1844 – only 10 years after the abolition of slavery. The detailed tripartite entrance and dressed stonework is unique on the island. St. Paul's Anglican Church is a more modest structure built, rebuilt and restored over the years; its old cruciform plan and tombstones indicate an origin in the late 17th century.

Few of the streets and alleys are sign-posted, but Nevisians know their town and expect to be asked for directions by visitors. Charlestown was built in slow-moving times, and the way to savour its qualities is to join in and stroll through its streets. You can't get lost!

St Paul's Anglican Church.

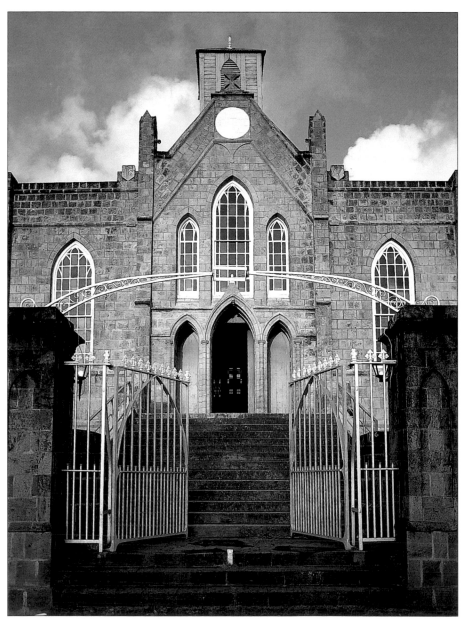

Methodist Church.

The Museum of Nevis History

The Georgian-style mansion housing the museum is built of volcanic stone and is the exact replica of the house where Hamilton was born in 1755. The house was reconstructed on the foundations of an old 1680 dwelling, which was probably destroyed during an earthquake in the 1840's.

On the ground level, there is a large exhibit hall displaying momentos of the island's history, from the Arawak Indians, to the sugar plantations, and up to the present time. There are also many artifacts and objects relating to the life of Alexander Hamilton. The second floor is used by the House of Assembly, the Nevis legislature.

Alexander Hamilton was born on January 11, 1755, (not 1757, as he claimed), the son of a Scotsman, James Hamilton, and a Creole, Rachel Fawcett. Alexander left Nevis at the age of eight and came back to St. Kitts in 1766. He was a bright student and had a real talent for numbers. At fifteen, he sailed off to

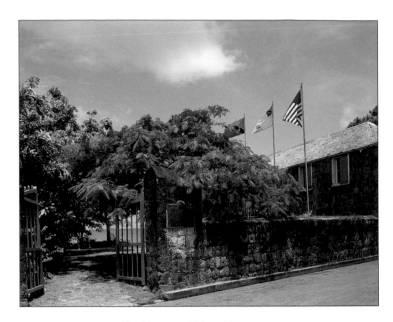

The Museum of Nevis History

America to go to school in Elizabethtown, New Jersey; he then went on to King's College, now Columbia University, in New York City. He was a patriot during the American Revolution, and became the first Secretary of Treasury under President George Washington. He was one of three authors of *The Federalist* papers, and was instrumental in shaping the political institutions of the United States of America: Executive, legislative and judicial. His most enduring monument is the preservation of the Union of the States as " one Nation under God, indivisible, with liberty and justice for all." His life ended tragically when he was shot on July 11, 1804, in a famous duel at Weehawken, New Jersey, with Vice-President Aaron Burr, of whom he had voiced a "despicable opinion", and died the next day. He left a wife and seven children, heavily in debt. He was not yet fifty years old.

The Nelson Museum

The Nelson Museum is housed in a white stucco building located between the Bath Hotel and Government House. It features a well-documented collection of artifacts on Horatio Nelson. Reproductions of paintings, engravings and drawings, old costumes and a variety of objects recounting the brave deeds and the love life of this extraordinary man are also displayed there.

Horatio Nelson was born in England on September 29, 1758, to Reverend Edmund Nelson and Catherine Suckling Nelson. His mother died when he was only nine. He joined the Royal Navy at twelve as a midshipman aboard the *Raisonnable* commanded by his uncle, Captain Maurice Suckling. At the age of twenty, young Lt. Nelson himself became Captain and took command of the frigate *Hitchinbroke* in 1779.

It was not until 1784, however, that Nelson made his mark in the Caribbean as a staunch enforcer of England's Navigation Acts. Assigned to English Harbour in Antigua for the next three years, Nelson established himself as a force to be reckoned with when it came to illegal trading between the English colonies in the Caribbean and traders from the United States. An early assignment, in command of H.M.S. *Boreas*, brought him to Nevis.

The culmination of Nelson's career in the region occured in 1785, when, passing near Nevis, he spotted four American ships trading just off Charlestown in violation of the Navigation Acts. He seized the vessels and impounded their cargoes. The Nevis merchants who owned the freight sued Nelson, but the Court decided in Nelson's favor.

It was at Nevis' Montpelier Estate in the late spring of 1785, that he met a young widow by the name of France "Fanny" Nisbet, and her son, Josiah. They fell in love and wed on March 11, 1787, at Montpelier, with the future King of England, Prince William Henry (William IV), giving away the bride.

Captain Nelson was assigned to the *Agamemnon* in 1793, and soon moved into the period of his life that established him as England's greatest naval hero. He had such skill at naval tactics that he has been called a genius by some. The "Nelson touch" refers to the many instances in which he was successful in battle. On October 21, 1805, off the coast of Spain near Cape Trafalgar, Admiral Horatio Nelson fought his most valiant battle. It was on this occasion that his famous phrase, "England expects that every man will do his duty", became a rallying cry for many generations to come. It was also the battle during which Nelson was shot, and died at the age of forty-seven.

200th Anniversary of the marriage of Nelson to Frances Nisbet.

AROUND THE ISLAND

Nevis is an island for connoisseurs. People come here to relax and wind down. There are no traffic lights, no jams. Only a few hours suffice to circumnavigate the 20-mile main road, even allowing for photographs and a picnic.
The road winds and twists through the uplands on the leeward side, past the parishes of St. John's Figtree and St. George's Gingerland, then down to the lonely Atlantic shore, past Brick Kiln, St. James' Windward and Long Haul Bay. Fields of sea cotton, dense coconut palm groves, forlorn ruins of sugar plantations, their machinery forever stilled, and the eerie shell of Eden Brown Estate, scene of an 18th-century duel, provide a running narrative. Tiny hamlets, bearing names like Chicken Stone or Hard Times, tell their own story.
Friendly minibuses ply the roads of Nevis, never failing to stop for a weary traveller, no matter how many passengers are already squeezed into the seats. They proudly announce their names in bold letters: "DEM SAY", "SMILE ON ME", "B' DARLING" or "GOSPEL TRAIN".

From Charlestown going north, the first stop is at St Thomas' Anglican Church atop a prominent hill. Originally built in 1643, it is the oldest church in Nevis – and may be the oldest surviving church in the English-speaking Caribbean. It contains a number of memorials to early settlers.
In the churchyard, the graves of planter families are oriented eastwards facing the rising sun. They overlook one of the most beautiful views of the sea. Further down the hillside, stands a school building whose roof was carried away by Hurricane Hugo in 1989, but which the Nevisians, ever anxious to preserve their heritage, are patiently restoring.
Continuing down the main road, one passes Nelson Spring on the right. The great number of artifacts found in the area suggests that this spring was already known to the Amerindians. However, its name comes from the fact that Captain Horatio Nelson supplied fresh water to his troops here in the 1780's. Opposite the spring is a beautiful mangrove surrounded by a coconut plantation.
A little further on the left, at Cades Bay, is Fort Ashby. It is one of the oldest forts on the island. Several cannons remain. The pleasant restaurant there overlooks a mangrove inhabited

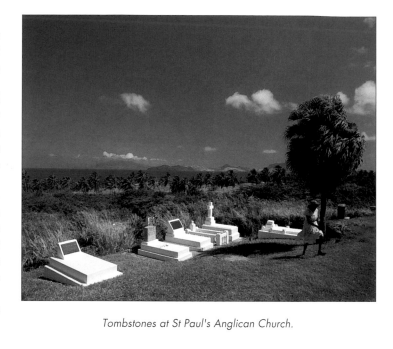
Tombstones at St Paul's Anglican Church.

by colorful birds of all species. Above the fort, climbing up towards the Nevis Peak, is one of several sulphur quarries. Steam sometimes escapes from fumaroles. It is a modern quarry which came into operation in 1951.

Continuing the main road towards the airport, right after a long stretch of straight road, there is a yellow sign pointing to the right. About 500 yards, up a rocky road, one arrives at the charming Cottle Church. It was built in 1824 by John Cottle, the owner of Round Hill Estate which, at the time, covered an area of 980 acres. Cottle was President of Nevis and known as a gentle slavemaster. He built the church as a place of worship for his family and slaves, as the latter were not allowed to belong to any of the Anglican churches at the time. Unfortunately, erosion has by now badly damaged the structure.

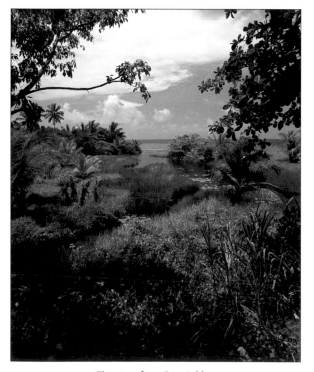
The view from Fort Ashby.

Just past the airport on the left is the Newcastle Redoubt, which was used as a shelter during naval attacks, and as a defensive fortification – evident from its thick walls, small openings for guns, former upper floor, and attached cistern. It is shown on a 1703 map, but its construction techniques suggest that it is probably older.

Still in Newcastle, beyond the police station, stands a long grey concrete building. It is the Nevis Pottery Factory, where all kinds of useful and decorative wares are made by hand, according to traditional methods. The clay comes from the nearby Potworks Estate, and the unique red color is obtained by adding crushed rock. The objects are fired over a bonfire fueled by coconut shells.

A few kilometers farther down the main road is St James' Anglican Church. Built in the late 17th century, its earliest tombstone dates back to 1679. It is one of three churches in the Caribbean known to contain a black crucifix. The sanctuary floor contains many stone crypts where early Nevis settlers lay buried.

Eden Brown Estate is located just a few kilometers further south, after Butler. Built around 1740, this estate is said to be haunted, after an incident in 1822. A duel took place between a Maynard (the groom) and a Huggins (the best man) on the day of Maynard's wedding to one Julia Huggins. Both men were mortally wounded, and it is said that Julia became a recluse. The estate was abandoned and eventually went to ruin.

The black crucifix at St. James' Anglican Church.

Eden Brown Estate.

New River Estate lies southward on the left. Built as a sugar producing and processing plantation in the 17th century, its machinery was converted to steam in the late 19th century and continued operating until the 1940's. The standing ruins of the main buildings are still in excellent condition, especially the windmill machinery and the cistern.

Coconut Walk Estate is located along a side road leading down to the sea. It is probably the sugar estate in the best state of preservation remaining on the island today. Some of the stone work dates back to the mid-18th century. However, most of what is left standing was built between 1810 and 1834. It has the largest sugar mill on Nevis due to its position at sea-level, ideal for collecting wind. The coastline is rugged here, and offers visitors a chance to see the contrast between the windward coast and the leeward coast, with its calmer waters and sandy beaches.

Further up towards Nevis Peak, on the right, is Golden Rock Estate, now an inn. Most buildings have been carefully restored, and visitors may ask Manager Pam Barry to give them a guided tour of the old mill which has been transformed into a honeymoon suite. An excellent plantation breakfast is served, with fluffy French toast a specialty. (Luckily, the kitchen staff doesn't keep count!)

Stonyhill Reservoir is close to the hotel. It is the starting point of a beautiful walk towards the main source of fresh water in Nevis. On the way up, one discovers the rainforest and its lush vegetation, colorful birds and butterflies, and, with a bit of luck, one may even encounter a playful group of Vervet monkeys. It is advisable to hire a guide for this tour, to be sure to see everything and to avoid getting lost.

Back on the main road, at the Nevis Bank crossroads, turn left onto the secondary road leading to Indian Castle Estate, now a government farm, where cattle and several experimental crops are raised. It was at one time a busy port, bustling with ships coming to load sugar and by-products for export to England, Canada and the United States. The racetrack is also located there along one of the wildest beaches of the island.

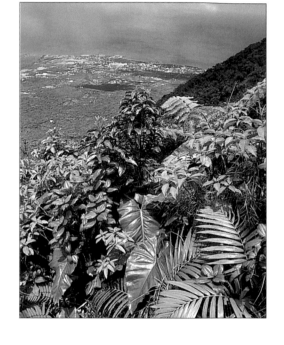

The view from the Nevis peak.

Sunshine at Coconut Walk Estate.

On the way back from Indian Castle, on the right, is St George's Anglican Church, built circa 1842, with additions including a major reconstruction in the 1950's after an earthquake. The basic layout is typical of Anglican church architecture, with two large entrances and a central worship chamber. The earliest tombstone dates back to 1724.

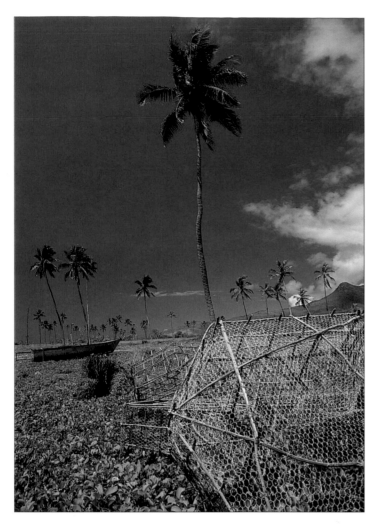

Fish traps at Indian Castle Beach.

St George's Anglican Church.

The Gingerland Methodist Church, dating from 1801, stands after the crossing on the left. The present building, unusual for Nevis, was reconstructed in 1930. It is a Richardsonian-style octagonal shape, with intricate roof joists.

Saddle Hill is located to the south of the island. Getting there is difficult, however, and it is better to have a guide. A fortress, still in excellent condition today, was built in 1740, on a high promontory. Horatio Nelson is reported to have used this vantage point as a lookout for enemy ships.

Further down the road is a sign for the Hermitage Plantation Inn. Built around 1740, it is said to be the oldest wooden house still in use in the Caribbean. It has been meticulously restored by its owners, the Lupinacci family. An old cistern, water cooler and purifier, storehouse and stone walls can still be seen. The garden is very colorful and produces an abundance of tropical fruits during the season.

Opposite the Hermitage, follow the the road to the Montpelier Plantation Inn. This magnificent building of volcanic stone seems to have remained untouched by time. This is where Horatio Nelson's wedding with Frances Nisbet took place on March 11, 1787.

Back on the main road, to the right, is St John's Figtree Anglican Church dating from 1680. The present building, however, was reconstructed in 1838, with additional work done in 1895. The marriage certificate of Horatio Nelson and Frances Nisbet is prominently displayed here.

BEACHES

The island is surrounded by magnificent beaches, each endowed with its own character and special charm.
The most beautiful is certainly Pinney's Beach. The grey volcanic sand is very fine, and the coconut trees bordering the sea give an illusion of paradise. One is never disturbed by other bathers, as the beach is "endless". In fact, this is one of the Nevisians' favorite spots for family fun on Sundays and holidays. The Four Seasons Hotel is located at the very heart of this idyllic place. The bar offers visitors a wide range of delicious refreshments in a very elegant beach pavillion. Snorkelling gear and equipment for other nautical sports such as windsurfing, catamaran sailing, pedal boats, waterskiing, can also be rented there.

Pinney's Beach.

Colorful boats.

The beach facing Nelson's Spring.

Opposite Nelson's Spring, beyond the Coconut Plantation, lies another lovely beach. Multicolored fishing boats rest on the sand, close to a hut of woven palm fronds that Robinson Crusoe would have loved.

Going north from Fort Ashby is yet another beautiful beach with a view of St. Kitts. In this quiet setting, tourists can enjoy leisurely refreshments at a local restaurant.

Sunset on Pinney's Beach

The Channel beetween Nevis and St. Kitts.

Oualie Beach is also very pleasant and an excellent spot for snorkelling. However, because of the strong currents flowing between St. Kitts and Nevis, it is best not to go out too far.

The road linking Hurricane Hill to the airport winds along another tranquil beach.

To the north lies Newcastle Bay, with its superb beach surrounded by a charming and typical Nevisian fishermen's village. Offshore from the Nisbet Plantation Hotel, a coral reef abrades the sand into a fine white powder and tames the waves, turning the beach into a swimmer's heaven. Here, too, snorkelling is an enchantment. The east coast being rockier than the west coast – washed as it is by the Atlantic Ocean and its rolling waves – has wilder, more-secluded beaches.

Windward Beach, which lies behind the Indian Castle racetrack, is a spectacular spot where fishermen moor their boats

The beach stretching alongside Charlestown is also picturesque, with an excellent view of the island from Pelican Point. On market days, fishermen arrive with their boats full of fish, and sell their catch directly on the beach.

Windward beach on the east coast.

Newcastle Bay.

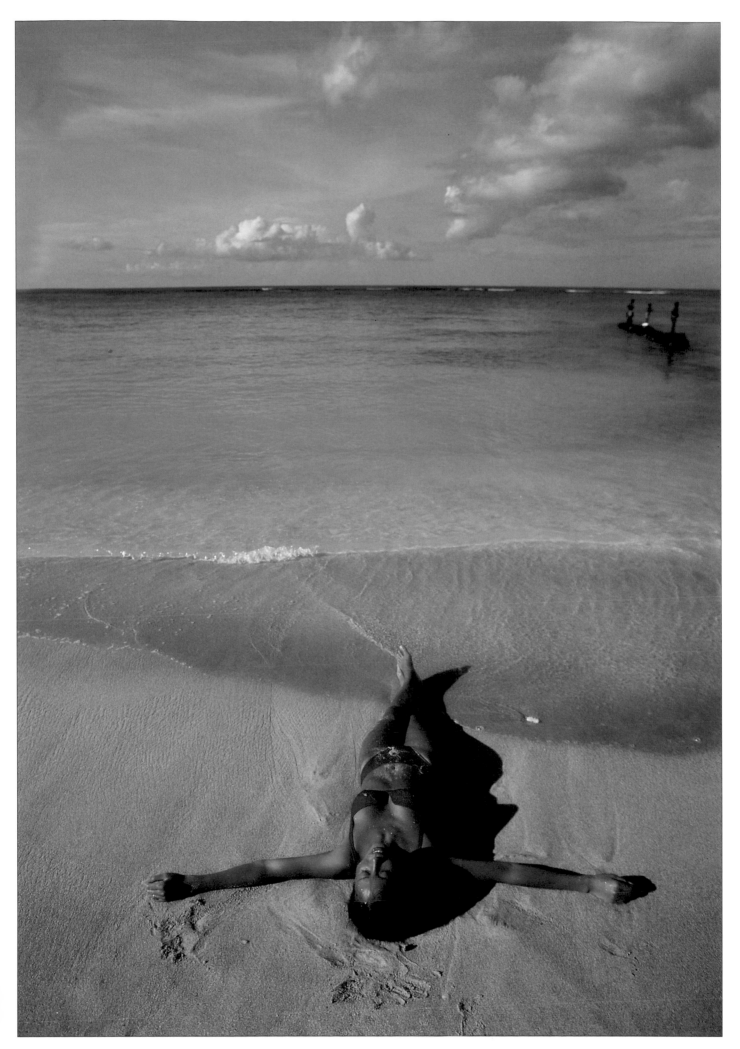

The clear blue sea at Nisbet Plantation.

SPORTS

Nevis is ideal for sports, whether on land, at sea or underwater. Every day a different activity can be enjoyed – the possibilities are limited only by your time and energy-level.
Horseback riding is a good way to start: you can go virtually everywhere and fully enjoy the island's peaceful atmosphere and backroads. Hotels organize guided trail rides for beginners, and gallops on the beach for experienced riders. The Hermitage Plantation Inn offers carriage rides to give visitors a taste of plantation life in the old days.

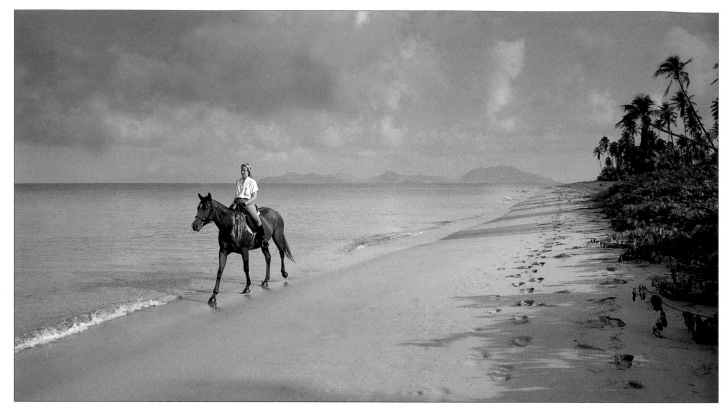

Horseback riding on Pinney's Beach.

At the top of the Nevis Peak.

Tennis courts are also available, mainly at the hotels. For instance, the Four Seasons has ten courts, as well as locker rooms where players can take a shower after a good game. The golf course at the Four Seasons is one of the most beautiful in the region. Designed by Robert Trent Jones II, this 18-hole, 6,766-yard championship course wraps around the resort and offers spectacular ocean views at every turn. For experienced players and beginners alike, this golf course offers challenges, from practice areas to a Black Tee.

For hiking fans, eager to discover the magic world of the rainforest, two thrilling hikes are absolute musts: The source, which is a relatively easy walk leading to one of the island's fresh water springs (the source provides Nevis with drinking water, so keep it pure and clean). The other hike, climbing up towards Nevis Peak (3,232 feet), is more challenging. During this four-hour-plus walk, hikers are surrounded by lush greenery, very different from the plants growing down below. Wear casual clothes and bring drinking water and cereal bars for a quick pick-up. On clear days, the view from the top of Nevis Peak is really breathtaking. It is the pinnacle of the island, and the 360 degree-view is unique. In order to ensure absolute safety, it is best to have a guide. Remember, there is no way of rescuing lost hikers, due to the steep slope and dense vegetation.

For those who like to spend time on the water, there are yacht charters: bare-boat, or with a seasoned skipper. There are also half-day sails to St. Kitts, with lunch and snorkelling included. Another possibility is to go deep-sea fishing with professional fishermen and try your luck with the Kingfish, Swordfish or Wahoo (gilt-head fish), which abound in the deep waters around the island.

The undersea world is magical in its diversity, and offers dazzling landscapes. With snorkelling gear alone, bathers can see colorful fish and shellfish, including rock lobsters, and even a large conch or turtle on the sandy sea bed. Nevis is also an outstanding location for scuba diving, but it is preferable not to go out alone. For additional information, call SCUBA SAFARIS which specializes in scuba diving, delivers licences and organizes outings at sea. Some sites are caves, carved by corals, in which divers may see an ancient shipwreck or an abandoned anchor.

The link between sports and a healthy population has always been very strong in Nevis. From earliest school years, Nevisian youth learn self-discipline and the rewards of athletic effort and teamwork. First among team sports is cricket, the undisputed favorite of young and old alike. Nevis has a tradition of great cricketeers, and has furnished

many valuable players to the world-Champion West Indian Team. In the regional triangle of Antigua - St. Kitts - Nevis, the trophy has been won by Nevis for the past three years. The season begins in early April and reaches the final play-off in June. Women's cricket is fast gaining in popularity.
Soccer and basket ball are also very popular spectator sports, played during the Winter season. Women compete in netball. Tennis counts a growing number of competitive players, thanks to programs in the schools.
Surely the most indigenous and "macho" sport played in Nevis is dominoes. From the male point of view this is the consummate game of swift thought , good memory and skill. It is also an occasion for serious male bonding, as the winning strategy rests on the mind-reading ability of the opposing partners. "Sincere dominoes", does not rely on signs or cues, which are considered to be cheating. The strategy is based on respect for your partner's hand, when he plays first. If an impasse is reached, you move ahead; and it is his job to help you maintain your position. Both try to" stamp out" the opponent at the earliest occasion. Scoring is by the number of points, often 1,500, or by the first team to win twenty games. Animated groups of domino players may be observed at favorite locations around the island. The brute force of "slapped" dominoes punctuates the concentration of the players, and four-letters words with a calypso beat send vibrations through the still night air.

SHOPPING

All around the island, one finds a multitude of attractive little shops offering an assortment of sundries and daily provisions: canned goods, household products, cosmetics, cold drinks and snacks. Conveniently located along the main road, they are often indiscernible from neighboring Nevisian houses with their brightly-painted wooden exteriors and corrugated metal roofs.

In Charlestown, one finds a larger selection of grocery stores, including several supermarkets which carry a wide variety of items from frozen foods to floor-mops to Dom Perignon champagne!

In the covered market, local farmers display their fruits and vegetables, as well as homebrewed beverages and freshly-picked coconuts to "drink".

Along Main Street, and tucked away in courtyards, are boutiques which feature fashions appropriate for the island climate, such as T-shirts, sundresses, skirts, sandals and straw hats.

Fresh papayas.

Shopping in Charlestown.

Caribelle batik, hand-printed in gorgeous colors at the Romney Manor in St. Kitts, is available by the yard or made into flouncy skirts with matching blouses at Island Hopper.

Another locally-produced label, Island to Island, is the work of Canadian top designer, John Warden. The collection perfectly mirrors the gaiety and breeziness of the Caribbean in a variety of beautifully-made dresses, skirts, ensembles and beachwear.

On Saturdays, merchants sell ready-to-wear clothing from open vans, flea-market style.

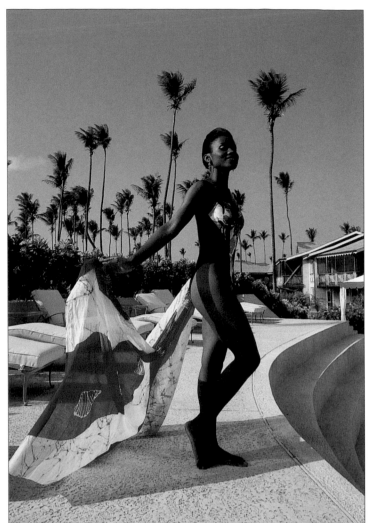

A model wearing a local fashion.

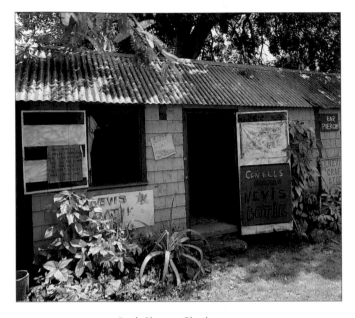

Batik Shop in Charlestown.

Arts and crafts of high quality are produced in Nevis; Newcastle Pottery makes fired ceramic objects from simple vases to crockery pots to naïf animals and figurines.

Local artisans have a knack for making amusing and useful objects from all sorts of natural materials, such as coconut husks and seashells. Nevis Handicraft Co-op, close by the Tourism office, offers a large display of crafts and souvenirs at reasonable prices: feed-bag garments; woven-straw purses and totes; wall hangings; wooden bowls and utensils; and delicious homemade preserves, jellies, chutneys and the ubiquitous hot sauce.

Fragrant honey from tropical island flowers is produced by Nevisian bees and their keepers and sold in local shops and confectionaries.

Hotels often have their own souvenir shops for the convenience of guests, but it is often more profitable to shop around for greater variety and better prices.

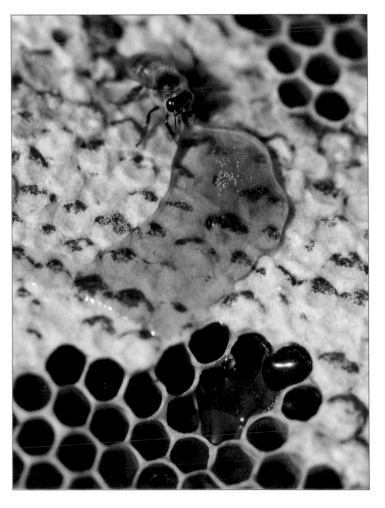

The tasty honey made from island flowers.

NEVIS-STYLE CUISINE

by Deborah Lellouch

Whether for a traditional West Indian family meal or local fare at the inns and hotels of the island, good cooking begins with a choice of Nevisian produce from the open-air markets of Charlestown. Homegrown vegetables abound: breadfruit and christophine, eggplant and okra, pumpkin and yams, plantains and pigeon peas, tannia roots, avocados, and peppers both sweet and hot. Homemade pepper sauces rival one another for flavor and heat. Being a vegetarian here would be no hardship, as these delectables are turned into savory casseroles, soups and stews, fritters, purees, salads, relishes or the hearty rice dishes which round out each meal.

Charlestown Market.

Almost every household, however, has a few chikens, a resident pig who conveniently consumes the table scraps, and a family of goats or sheep. Island goats and sheep are often indistinguishable to a newcomer, but those in the know know; Goats' tails point up; sheep's tails point down. All these farmyard animals roam the countryside unfettered, eventually finding their way to the local butcher, and then to the cooking pot. Fragant curries, goat water, Saturday-night souse (pigs knuckles and trotters), smoky ribs, and versatile chiken-marinated, grilled, stewed or deliciously deep-fried in a crispy coating, are readily available. Reputations are made on "the best of" each specialty. Just ask a local!

Culturama, in late July, includes a week-long food fest on the waterfront to showcase culinary talent and sustain the calypso musicians and dancers through the night. The aromas are tantalizing on the evening breeze. Colorful stands feature meat or fish filled rotis, johnnycakes, spareribs, chiken or lambi (conch) to be downed with prodigious quantities of rum punch, Ting, or ice-cold Carib beer. Home brews include tangy ginger beer, sarsaparilla and maubi, prepared from tree bark.

Family of goats.

Chicken roties.

The water around Nevis still yield an abundance of fish; kingfish, hind, flying fish, dolphin and snapper. The ubiquitous salt fish (salted cod) arrives in solid slabs from New England and points north. Salt fish finds its way into fritters, roti and rice dishes.

Most often, fresh fish are manirated in spices and lime juice before being broiled, steamed or stewed in a savory broth. Cooked until the bones "melt", stew fish are accompanied by fungi (cornmeal and okra dumplings) and homemade breads for dunking. Pepper sauce is a must at the table. You may see a Nevisian pop down a fish head with good-to-the-last-bite gusto.

Succulent Caribbean lobster is almost an everyday indulgence in local restaurants, appearing in salads and sandwiches, or classically grilled with parsley butter. More exotic version include lobster baked in coconut milk, steamed with vanilla, or curried in stew. Fresh from the Caribbean Sea, this is a flavor and texture treat not to be missed by those of us accustomed to the frozen stuff.

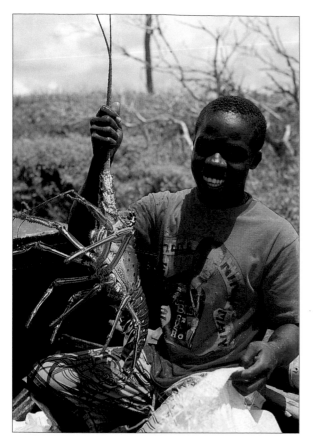

Lobster fisherman.

Glance upward into the trees for a visual foretaste of the dessert menu: mangoes, papayas, coconuts, sugar apples, oranges, grapefruit and bananas, ready to be consumed, as is, or to be transformed into fruit ices and creams, mousses and

custards, cakes and pies. A favorite with the kids are genips. They always know where to find genip trees growing, and spend hours in the branches sucking the translucent pink pulp off the pit. The green clusters can also be purchased from roadside vendors. Can one really overdose on this fruitful bounty? When sunsweet treats are there for the picking, anytime seems appropriate to enjoy these healthy snacks. And what could be sweeter than a freshly-cut stalk of sugar cane from a nearby field, juice running down one's chin? For the more sophisticated amateur, imbibe the native Cane Spirit Rothschild in a fruity concoction.

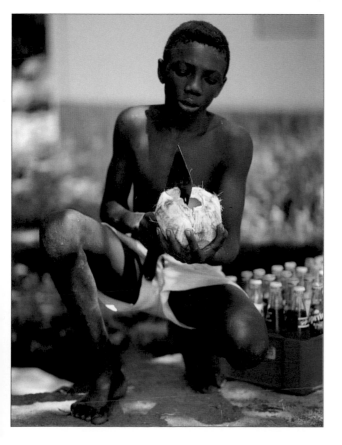

Pick-up trucks will appear wherever ther is a crowd, dispensing custardy fresh coconuts, opened with a flourish by a deft machete, providing both drink and food. Veritable staff of life for centuries in the Caribbean, the coconut palm was used for roofs, houses, rafts, ropes, cooking oil and soap, before making its way to the table. Puddings, pies and cakes, cookies and candies are just the beginning, as any pina colada fan will attest. Sweet savory, the coconut finds its way into Nevisian kitchens in myriad disguises, all the more appreciated since Hurrican Hugo felled many of the mature producing trees in 1989.

Whether shopping in the market or enjoying a meal anywhere on the island, it is easy to strike up a pleasant conversation with a farmer, fisherman, housewife or chef. You will tap a proud heritage of discerning quality, family secrets and plantation recipes passed down through generations. You may hear tales of the sugar mill estates from retired overseers or hurricane lore from lobstermen. Learn how to pick the perfect papaya or open a coconut neatly. Sample "bush tea" and rare herbs: culinary, medicinal or aphrodesiac. You may be fortunate enough to glimpse behind the scenes the good-humored bantering which pervades the bustling kitchen. Take time to savour the smelle, the taste, the colors of Nevisian cuisine, and it will whet your appetite for a lifetime.

Fresh coconut to eat and drink.

RESTAURANTS

The restaurants of Nevis cater to a wide range of tastes, depending on your appetite, your mood and your sense of adventure. From the ultimate in luxury dining, or a romantic *tête-à-tête* in the hotels and plantation inns; to a family-style meal served up in friendly surroundings; to a barefoot beach barbecue of fish, lobster and burgers – all are available for the inquiring visitor.

The Dining room at Nisbet Plantation,

and at the Four Seasons Hotel.

Beachcomber Bar and Restaurant - Jessups...469-1192
Blue Parrot Restaurant - Main Street - Charlestown...469-5996
Callaloo Restaurant - Main Street - Charlestown 469-5389
The Carousel Coffee Shop - Pinney's Beach
Cla Cha Del Restaurant and Bar - Shaw's Road - Newcastle 469-9640
Courtyard Restaurant and Bar - Main Street - Charlestown 469-5685
Dick's Bar and Night Club - Brick-Kiln..469-9211
Eddy's Restaurant - Main Street - Charlestown 469-5958
Fort Ashby Bar and Restaurant - St. Thomas Lowland...469-0135
The Four Seasons Resort - Pinney's Beach...469-1111
Golden Rock Hotel - Gingerland 469-3346
The Hermitage Inn - St. John's Parish 469-3477
Martin Entreprises - Newcastle Airport..469-9287
Miss June's Cuisine - Stoney Grove 469-5330
Montpelier Plantation Inn - St. John's Parish 469-3462
Mount Nevis - Newcastle 469-9773
Muriel's Cuisine - Upper Happy Hill - Charlestown...469-5920
New Castle Bay Marina Restaurant and Watersport Center - Newcastle..469-9395
Night-Cap Bar and Restaurant - Pinneys Ind'l site 469-0268
Nisbet Plantation Beach Club - Newcastle..469-9325
Nook Tavern and Restaurant - The Waterfront - Charlestown 469-5470
Old Manor Estate - Gingerland...469-3445
Oualie Beach Hotel - Oualie Beach..469-9735
Pemo's Restaurant - Camps Village..469-9188
Pinney's Beach Hotel - Charlestown...469-5207
The S's - Newcastle 469-9458
Scene II - Newcastle 469-9211
Sea Spawn - Charlestown 469-5239
Unella's Bar and Restaurant - Waterfront - Charlestown 469-5574

CRONEY'S OLD MANOR ESTATE

P.O. Box 70 - Charlestown, Nevis, West Indies - Tel.: (809) 469-3445 - Fax: (809) 469-3388 - Reservations: 1 - 800 - 892-7093

The original machinery of the Estate.

Old Manor Estate Hotel is located high on the slopes of Mt. Nevis in the Parish of St. George, in an area so lovingly called Gingerland. A ten-acre retreat of tropical gardens with fifteen guest rooms and a restaurant, all built within the restored stone ruins of the old sugar estate buildings. The old plantation's main water cistern has been restored to a unique round fresh-water pool, and the carriage house deck has been transformed into a tropical Jacuzzi for the comfort and enjoyment of guests.

The estate is owned by the Knorr family: mother, Vicki, and sons, Glenn and Greg, who, along with their staff, personally attend to the needs of their guests. The restaurant features fine dining in the casual atmosphere of the restored molasses warehouse and barrel-makers workshop, featuring an extensive variety of menu selections to suit all tastes.

Whether you hike to the rain forests or explore the many bridle paths and old plantation roads from the back of a horse, the scene is set to go back in time for a romantic, uncomplicated experience of life in the Caribbean at a slower place.

A spacious room in the main building.

GOLDEN ROCK ESTATE

P.O. Box 493, Charlestown, Nevis, West Indies -Tel.: 469-3346 - Fax: 469 2113 - Reservations: 1 - 800 - 223-9815

*Eva Wilkin
painting.*

The bridal suite inside the restored mill.

Follow the narrow drive that winds through a grove of mango, breadfruit and banana trees, past the hollow draped with vines where vervet monkeys play, and enter a world of breathtaking beauty and gracious hospitality.

The feeling here is "cared for", be it the original sugar mill cum bridal suite, built in 1801, by Manager Pam Barry's ancestor, the seven secluded cottages filled with antiques and Nevisian artwork, the greathouse with its bounteous *table d'hôte* of local specialties, the shaded terrace with its view to faraway isles, the spring-fed pool that mirrors the turquoise sea, or the tennis court. Of particular note, are the many original paintings by portraitist, Eva Wilkin, which grace the stone walls of the dining area and library. Additional works of this famous artist and lifelong resident can be seen at nearby Clay Ghaut. Most cared-for of all are the guests themselves. Virtually any request will be met by the helpful and informative staff.

In keeping with the island, activities are convivial and low-key. Guests are invited to participate in eco-rambles to the ruins of Coconut Walk Estate to learn about the history, archeology and ecology of Nevis, musical evenings with a string band, "the Honeybees", craft days with local artisans, or self-guided hikes through the cloud forest to the Source. Afternoon tea and homemade cakes, or a soothing rum punch, always await the traveler. Golden Rock maintains its own outdoor restaurant at Pinney's Beach.

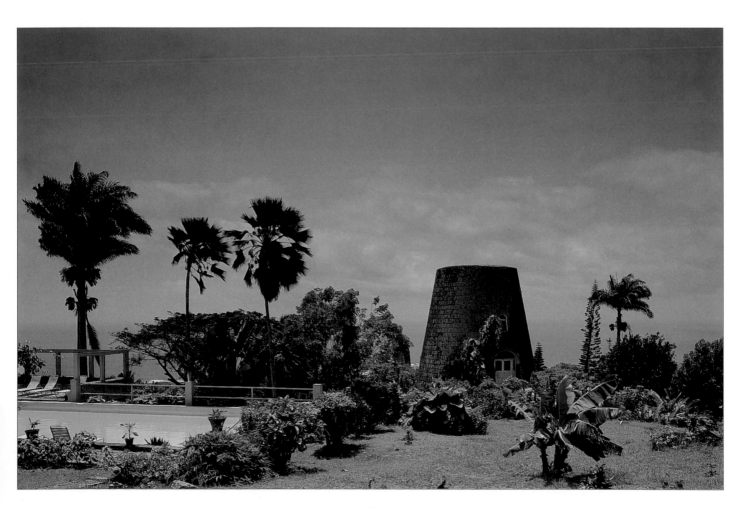

THE HERMITAGE

Gingerland, Nevis, West Indies - Tel.: (809) 469-3477 - Fax: (809) 469-2481 - Reservations: 1 - 800 - 742-4276

The Main House at Hermitage was built sometime between 1680 and 1740. Nevis Island lore calls it the oldest house on the island, and Jack Bertholet, author of the 1984 book, _Caribbean Style_, declares it the oldest surviving wooden house in the Caribbean. In twenty years of studying Caribbean architecture from Surinam to Cuba he had never found an older wooden house.

It was built as a small farmhouse before the days of large sugar plantations. The original owners were the Pembertons from Pembroke in Wales who likely experimented with various crops such as indigo, tobacco, cotton, spices and, eventually, sugar.

It was a small plantation of less than 100 acres situated 800 feet above sea-level. The land is stoney and strewn with boulders, with good soil in between. It was terraced into beds for cultivation, the extensive dry-stone walling remains one of the features of the plantation. There is no evidence of a sugar mill or factory, but there was a small animal-powered mill for grinding cane with horses, mules or oxen.

The strength and longevity of the house are due to the uncommonly strong mortice and tenon construction (heavily pegged at all joints), steep roof pitch design and extraordinarily durable lignum vitae timber framing. These heavy beams may have come from original Nevis trees, now extinct.

The property would have originally included the Main House, stone kitchen and ovens, water cooler and cisterns and other dependencies. The Main House is essentially as it was in the days when Nelson and Hamilton resided on the island.

In later years, the family prospered to own other estates all the way to the sea, and the original house was kept as a hillside residence for invalid members of the family. It passed from the Pembertons to the Maynards of Nevis in 1948, and in 1971, to the present owners.

Today, the Hermitage is a plantation inn and continues to offer traditional island hospitality and lifestyle for up to twenty-eight guests. The property reflects the owners' interests in island life with its original cuisine, reconstructed cottage rooms, collection of antiques, old-fashioned gardens, horses, carriages and local crafts and arts. It has become a "must see" for every visitor to the island. As a unique owner-operated hotel, it has recently been selected to be a member of the prestigious Romantik Hotels group.

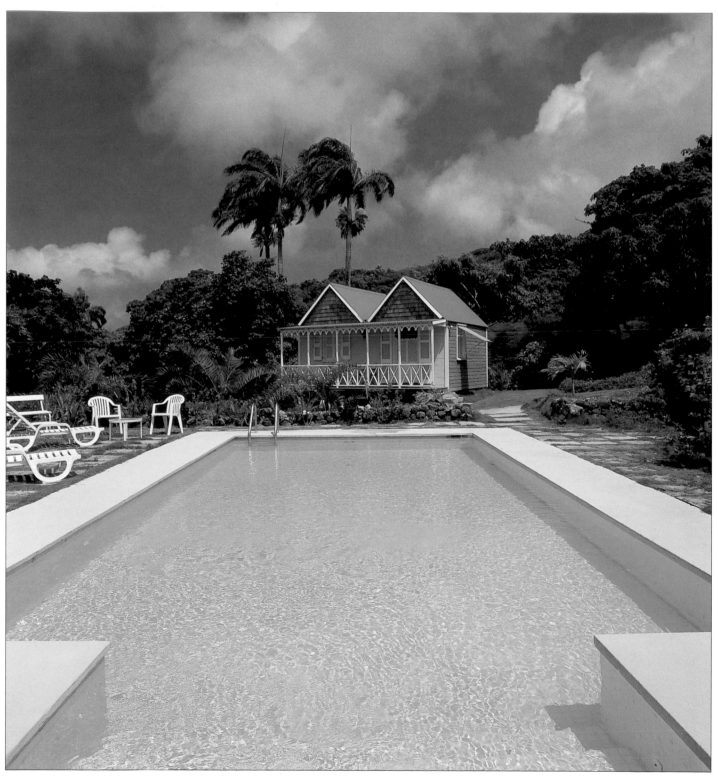

MONTPELIER PLANTATION INN

P.O. Box 474, Charlestown, Nevis, West Indies - Tel.: (809) 469-3462 - Fax: (809) 469-2932 - Reservations: 1 - 800 - 243-9420

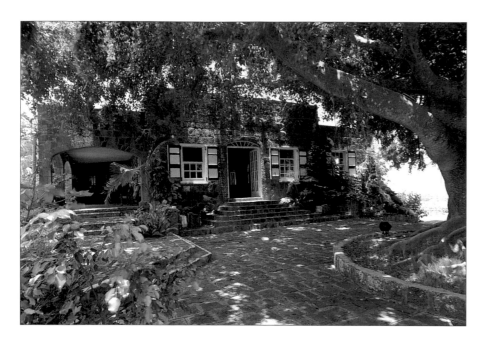

In the Seventeenth and Eighteenth centuries the plantations on the lush volcanic island of Nevis grew sugar cane. One such was Montpelier, named after Montpellier, France, by an exiled Huguenot who, after the revocation of the Edict of Nantes in 1685, had found life in his hometown untenable. Today the Plantation grows no cane and the buildings have been converted into a top class resort inn, small and exclusive. The French connection is not now so strong; Montpelier is owner-managed by an English couple, James and Celia Gaskell; but French is spoken, the wines are from France and various French influences are at work in the kitchen.

The main house.

The aim of the owners is to give a good value holiday of high standard. They feel that what the guest wants is to be made welcome, to be treated as a person, to feel safe and comfortable, to experience a sense of calm and tranquility, to eat and drink well, to meet other interesting and amusing people, to find beauty outside and good taste within, and to have enough to do and be able to enjoy a range of Caribbean sun-and-sea pursuits. The result is that you find here a rare combination of luxury and simplicity, a place whose beauty acts as a tonic to the stressed, a most friendly and delightful ambiance, all in an English country house party atmosphere – a home rather than a hotel.

You may spend the day at the Inn's exquisite private beach on the Caribbean side of the island, returning to the cool and lovely gardens of the Inn for tennis and afternoon tea.
This is the Inn chosen in 1993, by the Princess of Wales for a family holiday with her two boys. It is a member of Romantik Hotels and Restaurants, the German-based group of small owner-managed properties of the highest standards.

NISBET PLANTATION BEACH CLUB

Newcastle, Nevis, West Indies - Tel.: (809) 469-9325 - Fax: (809) 469-9864 - Reservations: 1 - 800 - 344-2049

This historic plantation, built in 1778, is a rare blend of old-world elegance and modern tropical comfort.

In the Great House, guests may relax in the lounge or chat over a cup of tea. The main dining room on the veranda serves delicious meals in a very romantic atmosphere.

Bungalows are set on the green lawn in the midst of a coconut grove. Appointed with modern utilities and private screened balconies, they are extremely comfortable.

Down the tree-lined alley towards the beach lies a beautifully designed pool. Lunch is served in the informal "Coconuts" restaurant overlooking the pool. The beach, sheltered by a coral reef, is one of the most pleasant on the island, as waves break on the rocky barrier out at sea. The sea bed is covered with aquatic plants, and a great number of fish can be seen swimming in the crystal-clear waters.This is an ideal place for those who need to break away from their busy and stressful lives.

The coral sand beach.

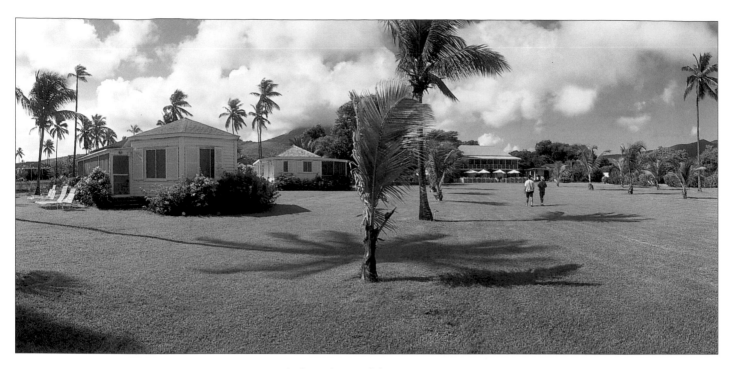

The bungalows and the Great House.

The pool restaurant.

Hibiscus.

HURRICANE COVE BUNGALOWS

Oualie Beach, Nevis, West Indies - Tel.: (809) 469-9462 - Fax : (809) 469-9462 - Reservations: (303) - 626-5575

The wooden bungalows on Hurricane Hill.

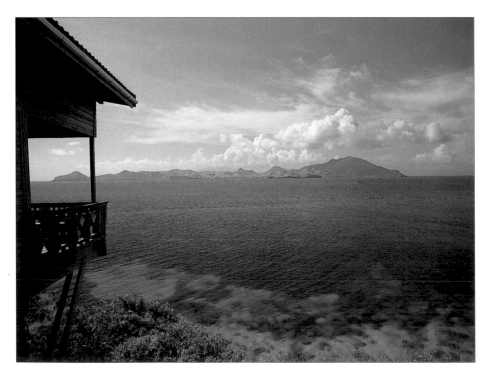

The view towards St. Kitts.

This attractive complex seems to be clinging to the side of a small hill overlooking the sea, and offers an exceptional view of St. Kitts.

The self-catering bungalows are made of beautifully hand-finished wood with tile roofs and floors, are tastefully decorated and include a fully-equipped kitchen, and covered porch. The Caribbean spirit can be felt in the decor of rooms, be they equipped with a queen-size bed or twin beds.

The French windows and shutters, and the hanging plants provide such harmonious touches that one feels as if the hotel has always been there.

The pool, built in the foundations of a 250 year-old fortification, seems to be floating between sky and sea. The beach is only three minutes away, by foot, and is equipped with facilities for nautical sports.

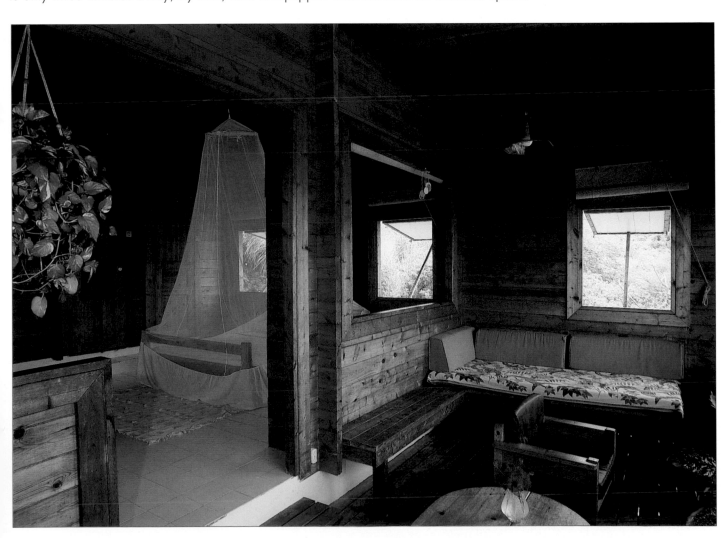

MOUNT NEVIS HOTEL AND BEACH CLUB

P.O. Box 494, Charlestown, Nevis, West Indies - Tel.: (809) 469-9373 - Fax: (809) 469-9375 - Reservations: 1 - 800 - 75-NEVIS

The hotel overlooks the small fishing village of Newcastle and is close to the ruins of Cottle Church. Built high on a hill, it offers a spendid view of the sea and St. Kitts, and an absolutely peaceful and quiet setting.

Its tranquillity and modern facilities make it an ideal place to relax. All thirty-two rooms are equipped with air-conditioning, touch-tone telephones, cable TV and VCR. Each apartment has a kitchen, and a private balcony where guests can have breakfast while enjoying the breathtaking view.

The main building includes a fine restaurant serving Continental and Caribbean cuisine. Down below is a large and beautiful swimming pool, which allows sunbathing all day long.

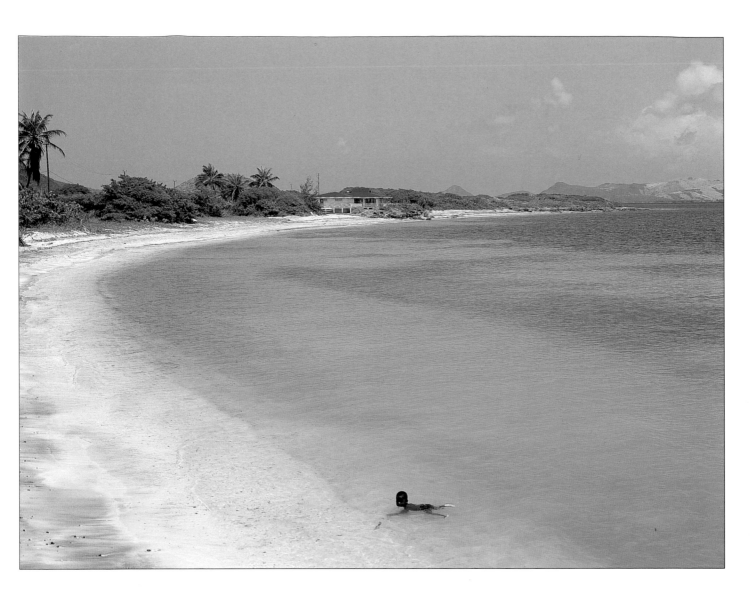

Down towards the sea, a few minutes from the hotel, is the Beach Club on superb Newcastle Beach. It is a pleasant place to have lunch or dinner, or simply enjoy a cocktail. Those who prefer to be more active can rent windsurfing boards or snorkeling gear.

OUALIE BEACH HOTEL

Oualie Beach, Nevis, West Indies - Tel.: (809) 469-9735 - Fax: (809) 469-9176 - Reservations: 1 - 800 - 682-5431

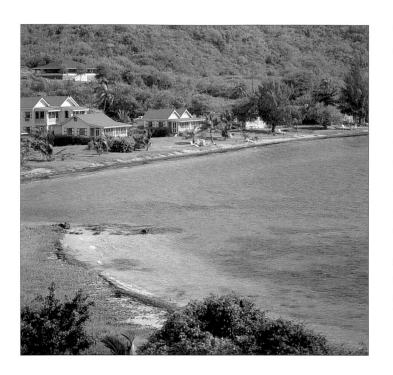

This lovely small hotel, built in typical Caribbean-style architecture, is located on a superb beach.

It is made up of bungalows, each with a private terrace overlooking the sea – just a few yards away from the beach across a lush garden.

The kitchenette, bathroom and other facilities are so cosy that guests really feel at home in their bungalows.

The restaurant offers Continental-style and Carribean meals served on a shaded terrace or on the veranda, according to the guests' wishes.

One could spend the entire day wading in the beautiful turquoise water. However, beach activities include scuba diving lessons, snorkeling, fishing and boating. The hotel maintains its own dive shop.

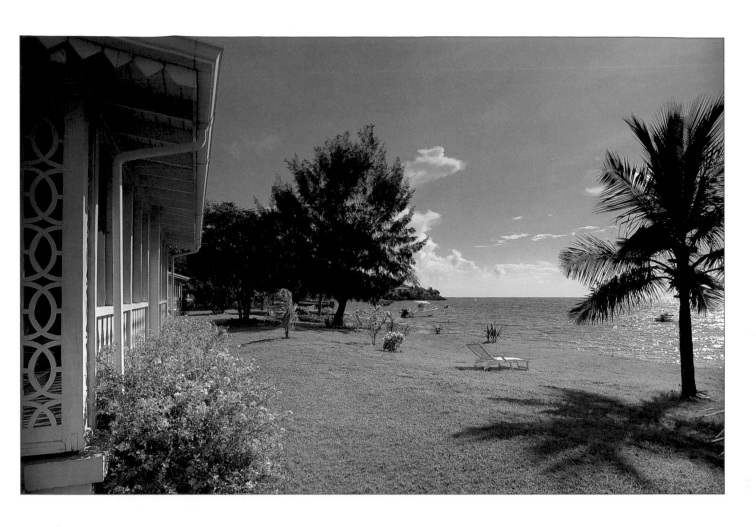

Private cottage in the Caribbean style.

Yellow Allamanda.

PINNEY'S BEACH HOTEL

P.O. Box 61, Charlestown, Nevis, West Indies - Tel.: 469-5207 - Fax: 469-1088

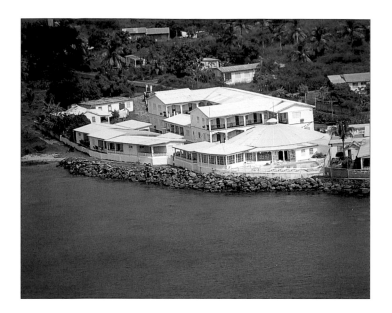

Built on the island's most beautiful beach, the hotel offers a choice of rooms with balconies or cottages with a private patio. Both facilities are modern and comfortable, and afford an exceptional view of St. Kitts and the ocean.

Enjoying the sun, or relaxing while sipping a cocktail by the swimming pool, are pleasures not to be overlooked.

In the evening, the chef prepares fine Continental and American meals as well as local seafood specialities. Groups are cordially invited for evening events.

Located at the water's edge, the hotel can organize any nautical activity offered on the island. Tennis courts are also available.
Downtown Charlestown, with its shops and sightseeing attractions, is just a few minutes away by foot.

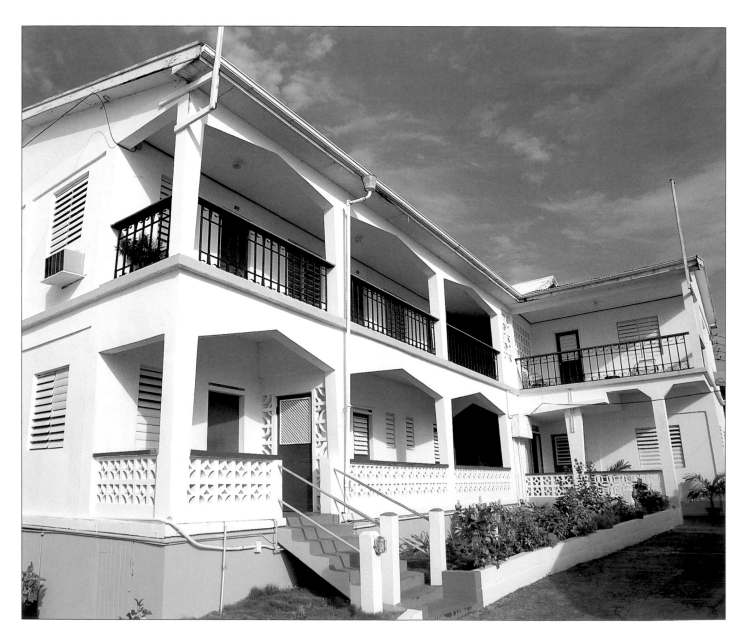

On the way to the beach along Pinney's road.

The pool facing the ocean.

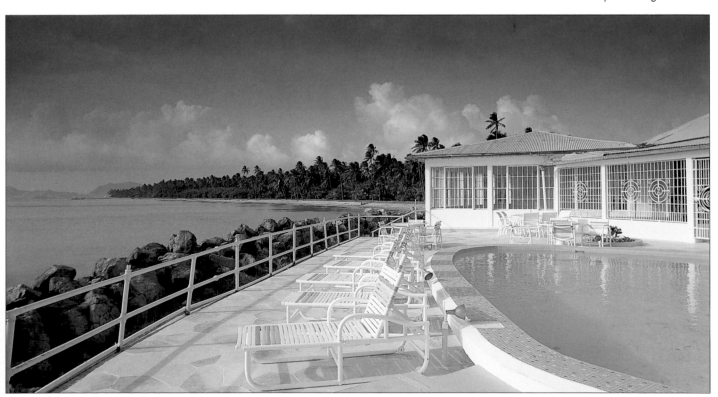

FOUR SEASONS RESORT

P.O. Box 565, Charlestown, Nevis, West Indies - Tel.: 469-1111 - Fax: 469-1112 - Reservations: 1 - 800 - 332-3442

By Brenda Fine

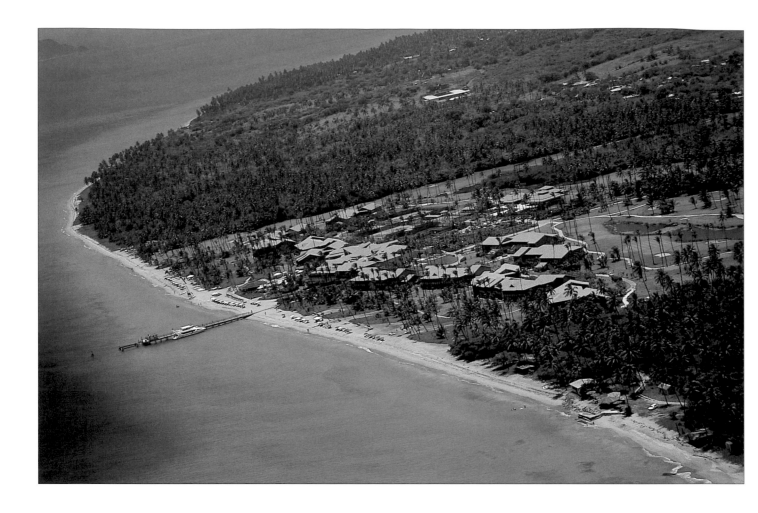

Caribbean resorts tend to reflect the style of their host island. If it's an island with a large city, expect to find big brassy casino hotels with glittery nightclubs and lots of partying. On islands that are popular with mainstream tourism and tour groups, it's not unusual to find dozens of cookie cutter hotels crowded along a single stretch of beach. And, on many of those undiscovered isles it can be hard to find accommodations at all.

How, then, to explain the exuberant luxury of the Four Seasons Resort on the quaint island of Nevis?

How to explain the delightful dichotomy of a world-class resort that has managed to blend in so seamlessly with its surroundings?

Explanations won't help. No matter how thoroughly one has read the guide books or has done his holiday homework, the first-time guest at Four Seasons Nevis simply cannot anticipate the treasure he's about to discover. Certainly the American Automobile Association found it to be extraordinary, honoring the resort in 1993 with the Caribbean's first and only Five-Diamond Award.

After landing on the sister island of St.Kitts, (although some guests do arrive directly to the smaller airport in Nevis) guests board a private launch for the short ride to Nevis. During this cruise they are treated to a panoramic sea preview as the Nevis shoreline comes into focus : The graceful sprawl of the resort fills the horizon, underscored by the long stretch of golden sand of Pinney's Beach, and accented by the cloud-shrouded Nevis Peak which dramatically dominates the background.

It's a beautiful sight, a postcard-perfect sight. But, as well all know, beauty alone is hollow if it lacks a philosophy to give it substance. And that's where the Four Seasons tradition takes over.

Hospitality has always been the key element to any Four Seasons experience, and here in the islands that signature hospitality takes on a particular charm. Guests experience a profound sense of well-being which comes not from a fawning kind of pampering; rather, as the result of thoughtful consideration as to what elements contribute to a thoroughly enjoyable vacation.

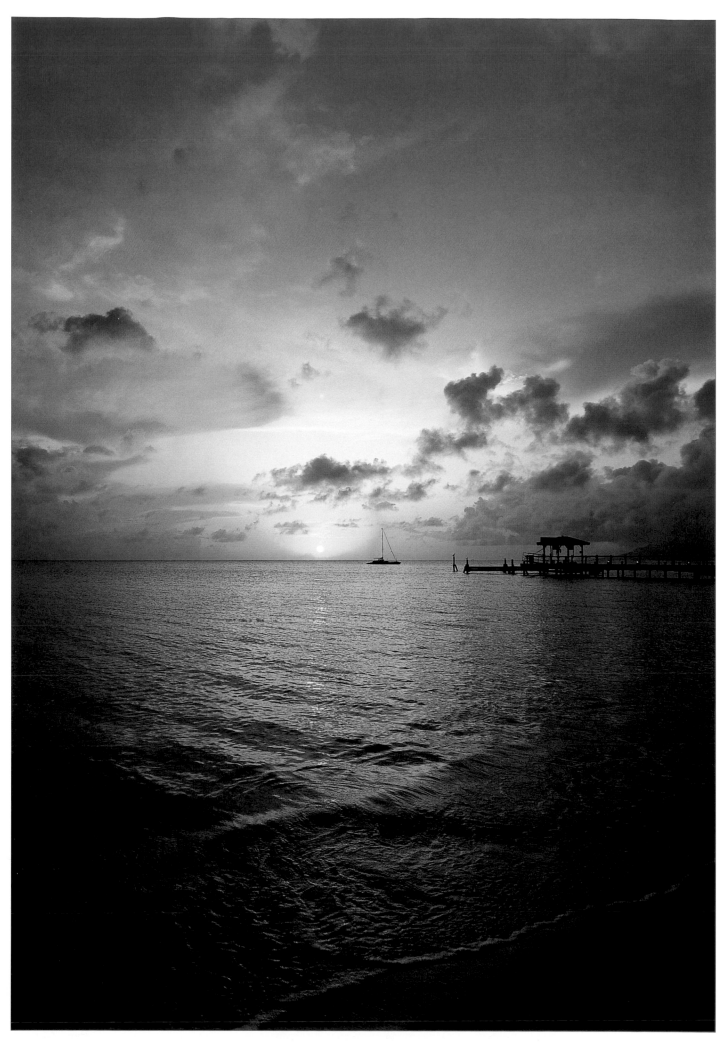

The pier where guests arrive from St Kitts.

No detail has been overlooked. No matter what the guest hopes to experience – whether it be luxurious surroundings, or days filled with sports challenges, with fine dining, or even stretches of benign solitude – it's all there for the taking.

Guests are welcomed personally, greeted at the pier on arrival, and escorted to their rooms in one of the two-story, West Indian plantation-style cottages which stretch out along the beach. All upstairs accommodations have large balconies; ground-level rooms open onto flower-bordered lanais. And all have glorious views, whether of the sea, or of the mountain and golf course.

The view on the ocean side.

The bungalows.

Breakfast on the veranda facing the golf course.

92

King-size bedroom,

Four Seasons accommodations are famous for their sybaritic bathrooms, and those in the Nevis resort carry on this tradition with generous abandon. Each marble-clad bathroom is oversized and features a deep soaking tub, separate shower, private toilet, and eight-foot marble counter with two vanities, and is stocked with all the deluxe amenities and stacks of fluffy towels one expects from a Four Seasons.

and bath.

Guest room are spacious, with living and sleeping areas furnished in the island's signature mahogany pieces which reflect the traditional English designs brought over by the early settlers. Armoires, beds, chests and chairs in dark woods provide graceful counterpoint for the soft sensuous colors of the fabrics, the exotic tropical plants, and the shuttered doors that open to reveal the lush island setting.

The Presidential Suite.

93

The Great House.

The architectural style of the resort recalls a time in the islands in which high ceilings and upper-floor balconies were designed to capture and maximize the cooling breezes. Roofs peak sharply to points, and frilly gingerbread trim softens all the edges.

The resort's Great House is a charming example of this West Indian-style tradition. Here, guests gather in airy rooms, or in the cozy library with its club chairs and shelves of books, for a chat or for drinks before dinner. Or, they stroll along the veranda which overlooks the inviting free-form pool below and the ocean beyond.

The Lobby.

The Nevis Yacht Club in the Library.

The resort's two main dining areas, the Grill Room and the Dining Room, both open onto this veranda with tables set for diners who prefer a meal with a view. Both restaurants feature international cuisine as well as an assortment of West Indian specialities. And there's always plenty of fresh lobster on the menu, thanks to the resort's unique lobster grotto which is located on-site.

The Dining Room.

The Grill Room.

95

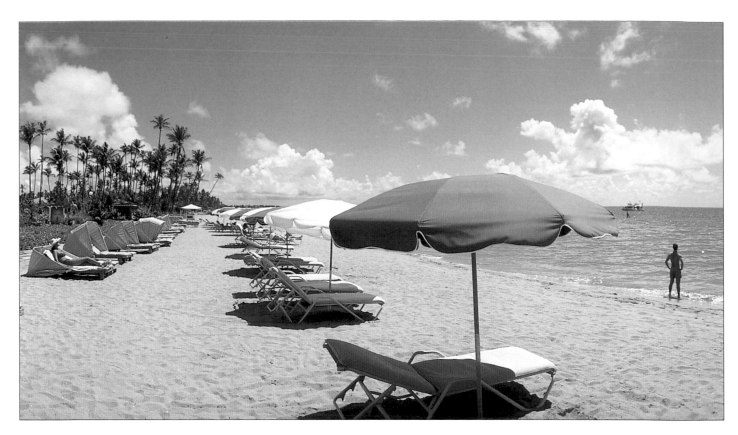

Pinney's Beach.

Sports-minded vacationers quickly realize they have come to the right place. The resort's golf course has been an island legend since the day it opened. Legendary not just because it's one of the few professional courses in the Caribbean. Nor is it legendary simply because it was designed by Robert Trent Jones II. It was his feat of turning an untenable terrain into a challenge, designing a course that hugs the side of the mountain. Outstanding among the many memorable features of this course is its 6,725 yard ascent up the volcanic slopes to the signature 15th hole which lies 420 feet above the sea with panoramic views that stretch all the way to St.Kitts and beyond. Golfers cover this mountain-climbing course in motorized carts, of course. And, because they are Four Seasons' guests, they can hail a passing beverage cart for some drinks, snacks and chilled towels.

Sunrise on the golf course.

The 18th Hole.

Tennis buffs, too, discover a similar mix of sports challenge and serious pampering. The resort's tennis complex centers around 10 hard surface and clay courts, which are lighted for night play and managed by the world-renowned Peter Burwash International. There's also a stadium court for the weekly matches and tournaments which are arranged by the tennis pro. Nearby, there's a complete health club with fitness equipment, sauna, whirlpool, massage facilities and a beauty salon.

All this activity is just a short stroll from one of the most beautiful beaches in the Caribbean. A beach where, as you can imagine, guests don't just sunbathe on the sand; they recline on cushioned chaises that feature folding canvas hoods designed to screen both sun and wind. Beach attendants hover nearby to deliver drinks, as well as chilled towels and perhaps a refreshing spritz of chilled Evian water.

Too much relaxation? Four Seasons' beach is filled with equipment for all sorts of serious water sports, as well as a remarkable assortment of water toys for the kid in us all. Guests can opt for fishing, sailing or scuba, or can play in the surf aboard oversized water tricycles and see-through rafts.

It's a total vacation designed to please the senses, amuse the intellect, challenge the body, and soothe the soul. Guests leave the island of Nevis feeling closer the nature, infinitely relaxed, and better equipped to plunge back into the real world.

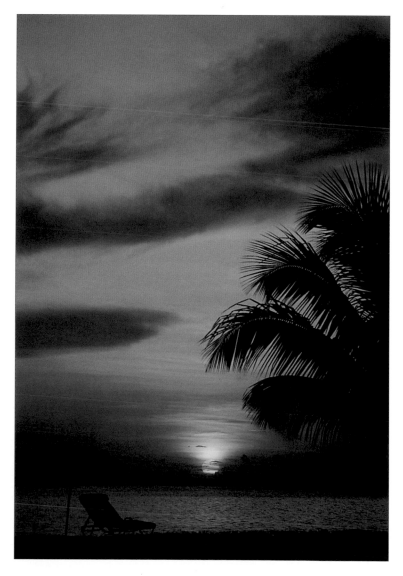

THE GOLF COURSE
Designed by Rober trent Jones II.

The Black Tee.

The 11th Hole.

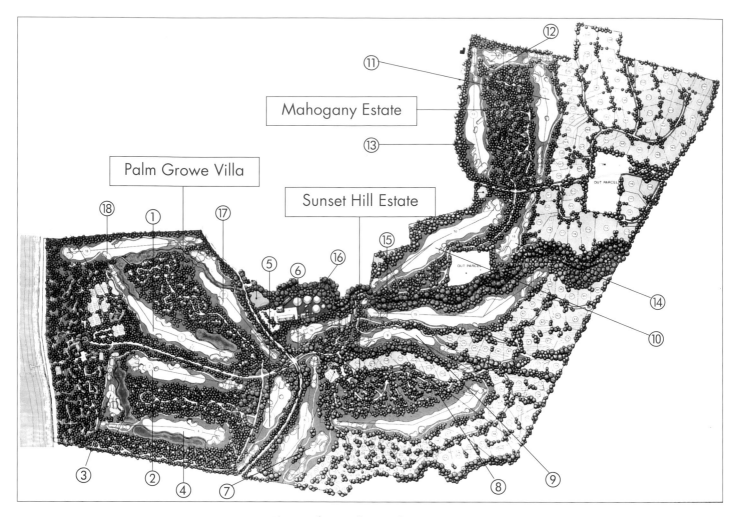

Mahogany Estate

Palm Growe Villa

Sunset Hill Estate

The view from a villa at Mahogany Estate.

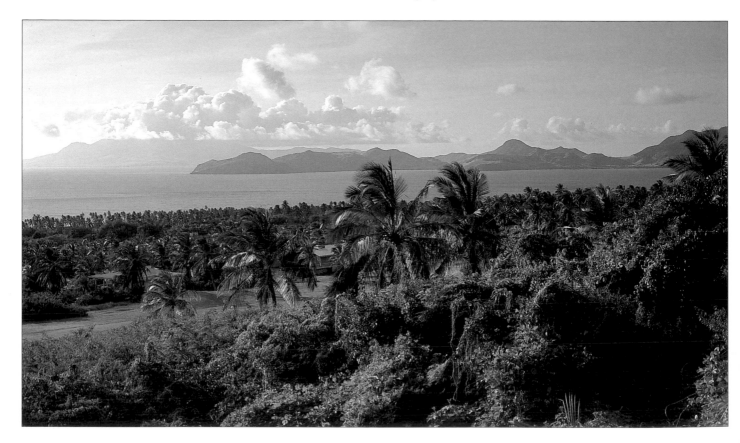

Between the white sand stretch of Pinney's Beach and the backdrop of Mount Nevis lie deep ravines and glistening rain-forest. Here are cashew, mahogany and mango trees and an array of hibiscus, poincinia and bougainvillaea. One of the islands oldest sugar mills blends into the distinctive landscape. Here, nestled in private enclaves amidst 350 acres of magestic palms and rolling fairways, Four Seasons Resort Estates will offers a superb collection of luxurious villas.

A villa of the Sunset Hill Estates.

Each home has been placed with care to take advantage of the magnificent diversity of scenery. Everywhere, the highest standards of gracious living have been incorporated in this stylish Caribbean setting, with meticulously crafted private residences reminiscent of the romantic style and grace of the old British West Indies plantation homes. Watch the morning sun rise over Mount Nevis from the Palm Grove Villas.

The veranda.

Enjoy the proximity of resort, pro shop and practice green, or stroll between the lily ponds along a pathway to the beach. The gentle slopes and secluded corners of Sunset Hill Estates offers stunning vistas and glorious sunsets. The mountain above, the sea below, but still conveniently close to the resort, beach and facilities. Toward the mountain, the land rises more steeply. From the spacious seclusion of Mahogany Hill Estates delight in the dazzling panorama of sea, sky, fairway and mountain.

The living room.

GENERAL INFORMATION

DO	DON'T
Greet people with "Good morning" or "Good afternoon", rather than "Hi". It is considered to be more polite.	Take anyone's photo (especially children's) without first asking permission.
Venture out on your own. You are safe anywhere on the island!	Be timid or standoffish. You will be missing a lot!
Slow down and approach people courteously. Life here isn't a rat race.	Be pushy. Haste makes waste, and puts others on the defensive.
Protect and respect the environment.	Disregard natural sites or dispose of trash carelessly.
Take up a conversation with the Nevisians you meet. Many are world travelers, just as you are, and share the same interests. All are knowledgeable about their island.	Be cliquish. Everyone here speaks English, although you may have to attune your ear, and listen closely at first.
Secretly admire the elegance and beauty of Nevisian women, the healthy virility of the men.	Overtly manifest your approval; discretion is the word. Nor dress skimpily in public.
Show you are pleased with the service.	Be patronizing towards service personnel.

HOW TO GET TO NEVIS

At present, Newcastle Airport in Nevis only accomodates small aircraft, due to the length of its runways. Most visitors will arive via Golden Rock Airport in St. Kitts, and make the five-minute flight to Nevis aboard one of the local carriers: LIAT, AIR ST. KITTS-NEVIS, WINAIR or charter company. Ther is also a regular Ferry service between the sister islands, and the Four Seasons Hotel runs its own shuttle boat, which accepts other passengers on a space-available basis.

FROM THE UNITED STATES AND CANADA:
VIA ST. KITTS, fly direct from Miami and New York, and from Toronto via Antigua. Flights to San Juan are available on all major airlines with connections to St. Kitts on American Eagle or Liat.
VIA ANTIGUA, direct flights from major cities on American Airlines, Continental, Air Canada and BWIA.
VIA ST. MARTIN, American Airlines and Continental Airlines fly direct from major cities. Winair and Liat scheduled service and charters connect to either Nevis or St. Kitts.

FROM EUROPE:
VIA ANTIGUA, Non-stop direct fly by British Airways and Lufthansa, and then by LIAT scheduled non stop flights or charters to Nevis.
VIA ST. MARTIN, non-stop direct on Air France, AOM, and KLM, and then by Winair or LIAT scheduled or chater flight to either St. Kitts or Nevis.
VIA GUADELOUPE OR MARTINIQUE, Air France and other European Companies have many flights every day, then Winair, LIAT, and charter companies to Nevis.
VIA MIAMI, non- stop direct on British Airways, American Airlines, Lufthansa and major European airlines, then by BWIA scheduled service to St. Kitts.

FROM ASIA:
VIA DALLAS, non-stop direct on American Airlines, United Airlines and Japan Airways, then American Airlines scheduled flights to San Juan. American Eagle and LIAT connect to St. Kitts.
VIA LOS ANGELES, non-stop direct on American Airlines, then American Airlines to San Juan and American Eagle to St. Kitts.

PASSPORT AND VISA

For a stay of up to six months, a visa is not required, for nationals of the United Kingdom, Canada, U.S.A., and Commonwealth countries, but suitable identification, such as a passport, birth certificate, naturalization papers or valid driver's license, and possession of a return ticket are mandatory. A valid International Certificate of Vaccination is only required when travelling from an infected area.

CUSTOMS

Personal belongings are admitted duty free. The following are also admitted duty-free: 200 cigarettes or 100 cigars, 1 bottle of spirits (26 oz.), and 1 bottle of wine, and a reasonable amount of perfume in use.
Cats and dogs are not allowed in Nevis from North America. They are, however, allowed in from England
- if free of rabies . An import license would be required for importation of pets
and is obtainable through application from a chief veterinary officer in St. Kitts.

THINGS TO BRING

CLOTHES: It is advisable to bring casual , light weight cotton clothing for daytime wear; bathing suits; a jacket or sweater for cooler evenings; light rainproof gear in case of a shower; and something dressier for dining out. Shirtless and barefoot dress is for the beach only. You will find attractive and appropriate tropical fashions in the local shops.
Hat and sunglasses are a must at midday, especially for children.
MEDICAL SUPPLIES: There are two pharmacies in nevis which carry over-the-counter and prescription drugs.
It is best, however, to bring along your own supply of special medication in case of ongoing treatment. Baby formula and diapers can be readily found in the local supermarkets. Sunscreen is an absolute necessity; the cool breeze is deceptive and masks the burning rays.
PHOTOGRAPHY: If you prefer to use a special type of film, it is best to bring an estimated number of rolls.
Remember, you will be tempted to take photos everywhere you go, at all hours of the day!
Photo shops carry the usual types of film and will develop them locally. Batteries are available, but expensive.

CURRENCY

The Eastern Caribbean dollar is based on the value of the US Dollar. The exchange rate varies from $ 2,50 to $ 2,70 E.C. for $1 US. Travelers Checks, U.S. dollars, and all major credit cards are accepted everywhere, except at the Post Office.

TIPPING

There is no obligation to leave a tip, but it is always welcome; and it is also a good way to show that you are satisfied with the service.

TIME ZONE

Local time is G.M.T. less four hours.

BANKS

There are six banks in nevis:
The Bank Of Nevis, Market Shop, Gingerland, Tel: 469-3564, Fax: 469-5798.
The Bank Of Nova Scotia, Main Street, Charlestown, Tel: 469-5411, Fax: 469-0231.
Barclays Bank, Main & Prince Charles Streets, Charlestown, Tel: 469-5467, Fax: 469-5106.
Development Bank of St. Kitts And Nevis, Main Street, Charlestown, Tel: 469-5416, Fax: 469-1262.
National Bank Ltd., Prince William Street, or West Square Street, Charlestown, Tel: 469-5244, Fax: 469-0194.
Nevis Co-Op Banking Co., Ltd., Chapel Street, Charlestown, Tel: 469-5277, Fax: 469-1493.

A WORD OF WARNING

The island of Nevis is quite safe compared to other Caribbean islands. However, it is advisable to take the following precautions:
Do not walk barefoot in the tall grasses or in the forest, as there may be stinging, such as red ants, centerpides or scorpions;
-Do not swimm too far away from the shore, as there are strong current, and sharks have been sighted;
-Do not sit under or touch the manchenil tree. The sap is very stringent, and can cause a burning sensation.
These trees grow near the beaches, and produce a small, green apple-like fruit.

TELECOMMUNICATIONS

Direct telephone, telex and fax services with all parts of the world are operated by:
St Kitts and Nevis Telecommunications Limited (SKANTEL).
A new system for direct long distance dialing is now in operation. Public phones are available on Nevis. Purchase your phonecard from the Skantel offices or from any other retailer. Cards are available in 10, 20; 40 and 60 EC dollar denominations. If you cannot find a number in the directory , dial 411 for a Directory Assistance.
For express mail, Federal Express and DHL services are available.
To make a local call : Dial the full seven digit number as listed in the telephone directory:
Nevis - 469 ....
St Kitts - 465.........

To dial an International direct call :
1- Caribbean nations with country code 1, dial 1 + 809 + 7 digits
2- To the USA, Canada, Alaska and Hawaii, dial 1 + area code + 7 digits.
3- All other countries, dial 011 + country code + area code + number.
Operator Services : 0.

Operator-assisted Internationals Calls :
1- To Caribbean countries with code 1, dial 0 + 809 + 7 digits.
2- To USA, Canada, Alaska and Hawaii, dial 0 + area code + 7 digits.
3- To all other countries dial 01 + country code + number.

To make Collect or Calling Card Calls :
1- From Home or Business Phone : to USA dial 111 or 0.
2- To Caribbean countries with code 1, dial 0 + 809 + 7 digits.
3- To Canada, Alaska and Hawaii, dial 0 + area code + 7 digits.
4- To all other countries, dial 01 + country code + number.

TELEVISION AND RADIO

All U.S. T.V. channels are available via satellite.
There is also a local T.V. station which carries local news and cultural programs.
Other Caribbean broacasting stations may be picked up in Nevis.
-ZIZ T.V. and radio in St.Kitts, tel : 469-2622
-Voice of Nevis radio, tel : 469-1616

TRANSPORTATION

Driving is on the left-hand side of the road.
A visitor's driving license is required and can be obtained from the Police Department.

Car rental:
Gajor's Car Rental - Bath Village - Tel : 469-5367 or 1439.
Nisbett Rental Ltd - Newcastle Airport road - Tel : 469-9211
Noel's Car Rental - Farms Estate - Tel : 469-5199
Parry's Car Rental - Pinney's Industrial Site - Tel : 469-5917
Skeete's Car Rental - Newcastle Village - Tel : 469-9458
Stanley's Car Rental - Church Ground - Tel : 469-1597
Striker's Car Rental - the Hermitage Plantation Inn,
offers bicycles, scooters and cars. Tel/Fax : 469-2654
TDC Rentals Ltd - Bay Front, Charlestown and in the Four Seasons Hotel.
There is an exchange arrangment between Nevis and St Kitts - Tel : 469-5690 or 1005

TAXIS

Ace Taxi Service - Water Front - Charlestown - Tel : 469-1973
Airport Taxi - Newcastle Airport - Tel : 469-9402
There are also buses driving all around the island, you just have to wait for one to pass.
It is the cheapest way to travel, but not the most confortable.

PHARMACIES

Claxton Medical Centre, Marbet Street , Charlestown.
Evelyn's Drug Store, Main Street, Charlestown.

TRAVEL AGENTS & TOUR OPERATORS

Air St Kitts-Nevis - Newcastle Airport - Tel : 469-9241 or 469-9064 - Fax : 469-9018
All Seasons Tours - Bath Estate - Tel : 469-5705 or 469-1138 - Fax : 469-1139
Carib Aviation - Newcastle Airport - Tel : 469-9295
Evelyn's Travel Agency Ltd - Main Street - Charlestown - Tel : 469-5238 or 469-5302
Jan 's Travel Agency - Main Street - Charlestown - Tel : 469-5426
Nevisian Travel - Main Street - Charlestown - Tel : 469-5423 or 469-5416 - Fax : 469-0487
Travel World - Main Street - Charlestown - Tel : 469-1460

GUEST HOUSES, COTTAGES AND APARTMENTS

Al's Cottages - Farm's Estate, P.O Box 201, Charlestown, Tel : 469-5426
Cabindish Villa - Newcastle, P.O Box 370, Woodbury, CT 06798 USA, Tel : (USA) 203-263-3750, (Nevis) 469-5901
Central Cottage - c/o Donald Hanley, Charlestown, Nevis, Tel : 469-5278, (Canada) 514-738-2255
Donna's Self-Catering Apartments, P.O Box 503, Charlestown, Nevis, Tel : 469-3464
Fort Ashby Beach Cottages, P.O Box 464, Charlestown, Nevis, Tel :469-5464
Headlands Cottage, Oualie Bay, Nevis, Tel : 469-9931/1581/5689, (U.K) 011-44-883-762107
Laurella's Cottage & Grove's View Cottage, Government Road, Charlestown, Nevis, Tel : 469-5623
Lyndale's Guesthouse, Charlestown, Nevis, Tel : 469-5412
Marisol Villa, Newcastle, Nevis, Tel : (Nevis) 469-9458, (US) 603-357-8321
Meade's Guesthouse, Craddock Road, Nevis, Tel : 469-5235
Pinney's Village Complex, Craddock Road, P.O Box 508, Charlestown, Nevis, Tel : 469-1811
Roundhill Greathouse, Newcastle, Nevis, Tel : 469-9233
Sea Spawn Guesthouse, P.O Box 233, Charlestown, Nevis, Tel 469-5239
Seastone Villa, Oualie Bay, Nevis, Tel : 469-9462
Sunset View, P.O Box 464, Charlestown, Nevis, Tel : 469-3464
Sylvia's Guesthouse, Ramsbury Site, Charlestown, Nevis, Tel : 469-5775/1899
Tamarind, Jones Bay, Nevis, Tel : (Nevis) 469-9549, (Canada) 416-781-2184

WATER

There is an adequate supply of drinking water for both domestic and commercial use, from mountain springs and sunk wells.
The Government has obtained assistance from a number of international funding agencies for upgrading the water supply
to stay apace of development needs on the island.

ELECTRICITY

The electric current is 220 volts, 60 cycles and 110 volts in a few hotels.
Some power failures of short duration may occur.

PUBLIC HOLIDAYS

The following days are observed in St.Kitts and Nevis as public holidays :

January 1 : ....New Year's Day
April (days varies) ....Good Friday
April (days varies) ....Easter Monday
May (1st Monday) ....Labour day
June (day varies) ....Whit Monday/Pentecost
June (2nd Saturday) ....Queen's Birthday
August (1st Monday) ....August Monday (Emancipation Day)
September 19 ....Independence Day
December 25 ....Christmas Day
December 26 ....Boxing Day
December 26 to January 2 ....week-long Carnival Celebration

HEALTH CARE

As developing tourism and related sectors bring an increase in the population of Nevis, new strains will be put upon the exeisting health facilities. New solutions will have to be found and financed.

The Alexandra Hospital, located on lower Government Road in Charlestown, is the island's only in-patient treatment center. Communities ara served by Health Centres, of which there are six. They concentrate on "family-life education" : preventive medicine and vaccinations; first aid; sexuality; dental hygiene; and caring for the elderly and shut-ins through outreach programs. They also report back to the District Medical Officer regarding any local health concerns. There are a number of task forces and professional associations engaged in family planning, aids prevention, mental health, nutrition, sports medicine, and diving sickness (Bends). Practitioners are expected to bridge any number of related specialities, while maintaining a certain standard of health care - and to make the best use of each resource, be it human or technical. In the words of Dr. Patrick Diaz, Chief Medical Officer for Nevis; "So much to do on a small island!"

The medical staff at Alexandra Hospital is competent, and devoted beyond the call of duty. It is comprised of two M.D.'s, trained at the University of the West Indies, Jamaica, and in the U.S and Canada; a Matron, who is an R.N, assisted by qualified nurses; mid-wives and pediatric aides; and laboratory technicians. Currently, there is no anaesthesiologist, radiologist or pathologist, which effectively limits surgery to minor procedures or emergency measures. Machine-assisted respiration is not available in Nevis or in St Kitts. This means that any medical condition necessitating major surgery or life-sustaining equipment, will be evacuated by plane or helicopter to hospital facilities in Puerto Rico or the Continental U.S. The Nevis Island Administration has expressed ongoing concern over these vital issues, and has begun to implement new concepts to ensure greater security. Among them, a disaster-preparedness program,
and an emergency air-shuttle using amphibious planes.

It is hoped the upgrading of medical facilities and equipment will operate a sort of reverse "brain drain", bringing back expatriate Nevisian specialists who have received their training and experience abroad. A forerunner of this movement, Dr. Eloise Edgings-Pryce, Medical Superintendant of the Alexandra Hospital, returned in 1991, to serve her countrymen after years of residency, fellowships and board certification in the United States. Coincidentally, she now heads the very hospital where she was born.

Alexandra Hospital.

Other areas of public health concern are testing laboratories for water quality and for environmental pollution, such as pesticides, used oil and chemicals. As the economy becomes more consumer-oriented, disposal of high volumes of domestic and industrial waste will require effective and foward-looking management solutions.
Given the high price of modern techology, and the subsequent burden to the public sector, users will be implicated more and more in the disposal process : from decision-making to recycling; from fee schedules to penalties for violations.
It is likely that certain segments will be privatized, and even turned into revenue-generating activities. Certainly, a campaign is needed to raise public awareness of the costs, over time, to the community, the economy and the ecosystem.

The Medical Library.

THE ALEXANDRA FOUNDATION

Established in 1989, by a group of concerned Nevisians, the majority of whom reside abroad, the Foundation has as its goal the maintenance and improvement of quality health care for the citizens of and visitors to the Island of Nevis.
A secondary objective is to encourage and support the pursuit of higher education, specifically, but not limited to the sciences and environmental issues, by those young Nevisians at home and abroad who meet scholastic requirements and possess the necessary personal character and maturity to successfully complete a course of academic study.
These goals are to be achieved through the tax-exempt contributions of monies, goods and expertise by Nevisians worldwide, and by friends and supporters of the people of Nevis.

The Foundation's vision of high-quality health care, for the island's resident and visiting population alike, has already begun to take form; medical equipment and training needs have been identified, and a plan of action have been drawn up.
A medical library and audio-visual learning center have been built on the grounds of Alexandra Hospital, and many books and journals have been contributed. Diagnostic and monitoring equipment has been received, and technicians are scheduled to be trained at Massachusetts General Hospital. Planning is under way for a medical symposium sponsored by M.G.H. and affiliated hospitals in Boston. A scholarship fund has been established in the name of Weston O. Parris, former Deputy Governor General of St.Kitts and Nevis, and revered educator.

An ultra-sound machine has been donated to the Alexandra Foundation by General Electric with assistance from the Four Seasons Hotel. The 3rd Annual Terry Fox Run/Walk, in honor of the brave young Canadian, to raise money for cancer research and the purchase of detection equipment at Alexandra Hospital, and a golf tournament has been organised by the Four Seasons.

Other hotels, including Golden Rock, Old Manor, Hermitage, Montpelier, Nisbett Plantation and Pinney's Beach, offer sizeable discounts to members of the Alexandra Foundation, some up to 50%.

Led by its founder, the visionary Philemon T.Walters, and fully supported by the Nevis Island Administration, the Foundation promises to be a significant partner in the development of quality health care, geared to the needs and scope of Nevis.

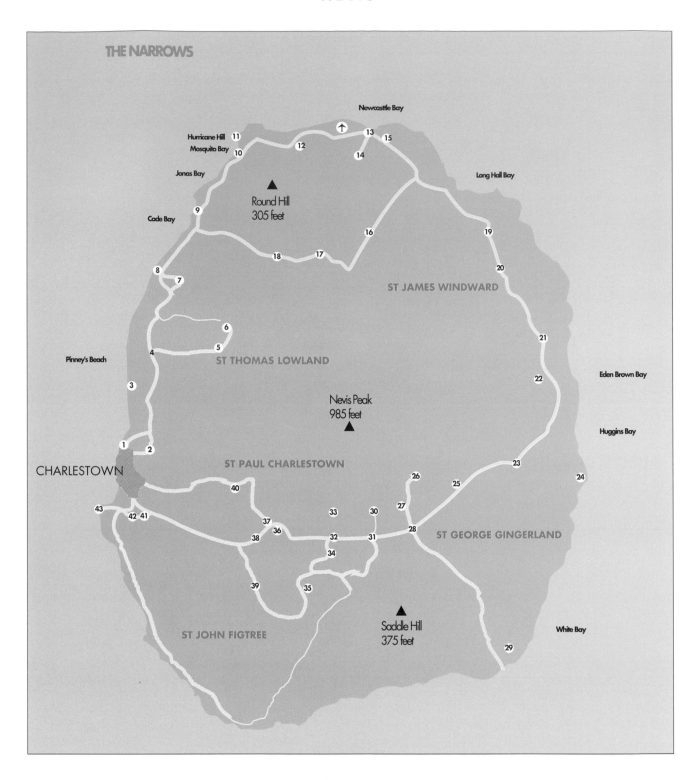

THE NARROWS

Newcastle Bay

Hurricane Hill   11
Mosquito Bay   10   12   13   15
  14

Jonas Bay   Long Hall Bay

Round Hill
305 feet

Cade Bay   9   16   19

  8   20

  7   ST JAMES WINDWARD

  6   21

Pinney's Beach   4   5   ST THOMAS LOWLAND   22   Eden Brown Bay

  3   Nevis Peak
985 feet   Huggins Bay

  1   2   26   25   23

CHARLESTOWN   ST PAUL CHARLESTOWN   27   24

  40   33   30   28

43   42   41   37   36   32   31   ST GEORGE GINGERLAND

  38   34

  39   35   Saddle Hill
375 feet   White Bay

ST JOHN FIGTREE   29

Caption

1- Pinney's Beach Hotel
2- Craddocks
3- Four Season's Hotel
4-Vaughans
5- Jessups
6-Barnes Ghaut
7- Cotton Ground
8- Fort Ashby
9- Cliffdwellers
10- Oualie Beach Hotel
11- Hurricane Cowe
12- Cottle Church
13- Newcastle
14- Mount Nevis Hotel

15- Nisbett Plantation
16- Mount Lily
17- Fountain
18- Westbury
19- Hick's Village
20- Whitehall
21- Butlers
22- Eden Brown Estate
23 New River
24- Coconut Walk Estate
25- Golden Rock Estate
26- Rawlins
27- Old Manor Estate
28- Market Shop

29 Indian Castle
30- Zetlands
31- Chiken Stone
32- Beach Road
33- Hermitage Plantation
34- Cole Hill
35- Montpelier Plantation
36- Morning Star Estate
37- Church Ground
38- Fig Tree
39- Brown Hill
40- Hamilton Estate
41- Government House
42- Bath Hotel
43- Fort Charles

CHARLESTOWN

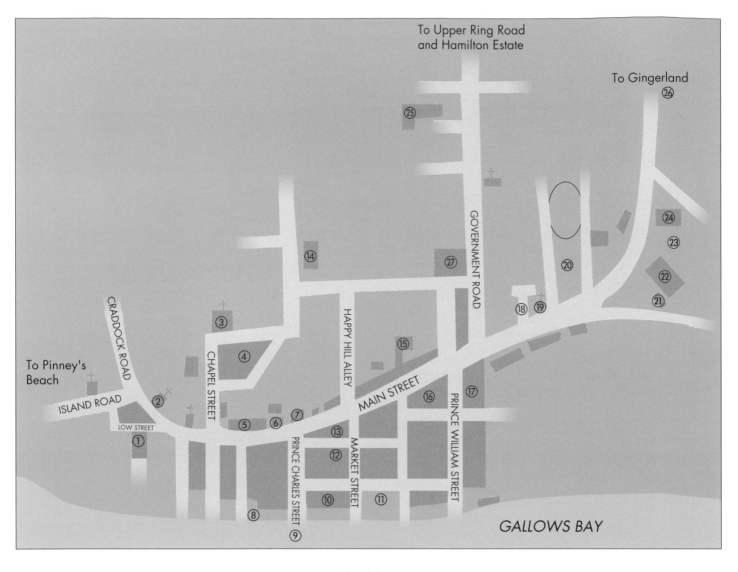

Caption
1- Museum of Nevis History and Hamilton Birthplace.
2- St Paul's Anglican Church.
3- Methodist Church.
4- Health Center.
5- Long Stone House.
6- Post Office.
7-Custom House and Treasury Building.
8- Taxi.
9- Pier.
10- Cotton Ginnery.
11- Market
12- Tourist Bureau.
13- D.R. Walwin Plaza.
14- Prep School.
15- Arcade.
16- Memorial.
17- Court House and Library.
18- Administration Building.
19- Jewish Synagogue.
20- Grove Park.
21- Bath.
22- Bath Hotel.
23- Nelson Museum.
24- Government House.
25- Alexandra Hospital.
26- Cemetery.
27- Jewish Cemetery.

BIBLIOGRAPHY

Geography

St. Kitts & Nevis. Environmental Profile, Caribbean Conservation Asoociation and Island Resources Foundation, 1991.

Nature

Beekeeping. The Nevis way. By Quentin Henderson.
Flowers of the Caribbean. By G.W. Lennox and S.A. Seddon. Pocket Natural History Series.
The birds of Nevis. By Paul Hilder.

History

Sword, Ships and Sugar. A History of Nevis to 1900. By Vincent K. Hubbard.
The Prehistoric Settlement Pattern of Nevis, West Indies. By Samuel Wilson - University of Texas. Austin - Texas.
Cottle Church - An Incident in the Life of Pre-emancipation Nevis. By G.P.J. Walker. Published by Nevis Historical & Conservation Society. - 1990.

Architecture

The Architecture of Nevis - A Short Analysis. By Daphne L. Degazon - Hobson. (1987)

Tourism
Brochures and Maps of the Bureau of Tourism.
Brochures of the Nevis Historical and Conservation Society.
Brochures of the Hotels.
The St. Kitts & Nevis Traveller. Tourist Guide bi-annual. The official publication of the Department of Tourism.
A Motoring Guide to Nevis. by Janet Cotner & Sunny Northrup. (1970)
The Island of Nevis (The place of birth of Alexander Hamilton) By Mary Pomeroy, illustrated by Eva Wilkin.
Nevis Queen of the Caribees. By Joyce Gordon.
The Settlers Handbook (Four Seasons expatriate managers).
Chrismas Sports in St. Kitts and Nevis, Our neglected Cultural Tradition, by Frank L. Mills, S.B. Jones-Hendrickson and lessons by Bertran Eugene, 1984.
Narrative on Chrismas Sports, by Oretius Jones, September 10, 1993.
Interview And Performance, Willard John, Moko Jumbie, St. Croix, U.S.V.I., August 1993.

General Information

St. Kitts. & Nevis Telephone, Telex & Fax Directory, 1993/1994, Caribbean Publishing Co., Ltd.
Four Seasons Resort Brochure.

PICTURE CREDITS

Photographs by Jérôme de Baecque
All the pictures have been taken with a Professional Camera: Mamiya 645.
Pages: Cover and 6-7-8-9-10(A & B)-11-12-13-14-18-19-24-25-26-27-28-29-30-31-32-33-34-35-36(B)-37(A)-38-39-40-41-
42-43-44-45-46(A&B)-47-48-49-50-51(B)-52-53-54-55-56-57-58-59-60-61-62-63-64-65-66-67(A&B)-68-69-70-71-72-
73(A&C)-74-75-76-77-78-79-80-81-82-83-84-85-86-87-88-89-90-91-92-93-94-95-96(B)-97-98-99-100-101-102-106-107

Photographs by Jean-Phillipe Godard
Pages: 10(B)-15-36(A)-37(B)-46(C)-51(A)-67(C)-71-73(B)-81(A)-96(A)

The Nevis Historical and Conservation Society
Page: 17

Independence Brochure 1983
Page: 3

Nevis Philatelic Bureau
Page: 55(B)

Archives du Musée de la Marine Française
Pages: 21-22-23

Archives of Pam Barry, Manager of the Golden Rock Hotel
Pages: 16-20

ACKNOWLEDGMENTS

There are many people to whom I owe thanks and gratitude.
Without their generous assistance, this book would not have been created.

The honorable Vance Amory, Premier of Nevis, and all the members of his Administration.

The honorable Colin Tyrel, Parliamentary Secretary, Youth, Community Development & Women's Affairs;

The honorable Franklin Brand Tyrell, Parliamentary Secretary, Tourism, Trade, Industry, Development & Planning;

Mr. Oral Martin, Director of Planning.

Mrs. Sylvie Alvarez, French Ambassador to Sainte-Lucie

Mr. Roger Garland, Executive Vice President of Four Seasons Hotels and Resorts.

Mr. John Stauss, General Manager of the Four Seasons Resort of Nevis, and his wife.

The entire staff of the Four Seasons Hotel, who contributed to the quality of our stay through·their kindness,
their availability and their unfailing help.

Mr. Denis de Baecque,Chairman and C.E.O. of Nevis Hotel Development Limited,
and Executive Vice President of LYONNAISE DES EAUX - DUMEZ.

Those who contributed their time and expertise to the realization of this book :

Deborah Lellouch, International Tax Law Specialist, who is responsible for the main body of written word contained
herewithin. She provided editorial guidance and overview from cover to cover, and infused these pages with her love of
Nevis and its people.

Calvin Howell, Director, Carribean Conservation Society;

Daphne L. Degazon Hobson, Architect and Historical Conservationist;

Eloise Edgings-Pryce, M.D., Medical Superintendant of Alexandra Hospital;

Glenn Knorr, Manager of Croney's Old Manor Estate;

James Gaskell, Manager of Montpelier Plantation Hotel;

Laure Mansuy, Geographer;

Pam Barry, Manager of Golden Rock Estate;

Patrick Diaz, M.D., Chief Medical Officer of Nevis;

Patrick Le Marec;

Philemon T.Walters, Director of the Alexandra Foundation;

Richard Lupinacci, Manager of Hermitage Plantation Inn.

Vincent Hubbard , Managing director of Morning Star Holdings, Ltd.,
and President of the Nevis Historical and Conservation Society.

All those who took time from their busy schedules to grant interviews, photos, or otherwise participate in this effort:

Mrs. Muller, DPE SOTEXI Company.

Mr. and Mrs. Peterson;

Sam Caines and his family;

Vanessa Paris and her beautiful children;

Quentin Henderson and his bees;

Mr. and Mrs. Smith and their daughter;

Luce Gerard and Philippe Than, Editions du Moniteur;

HomelCarib Aviation;

All our friendly models who cooperated with such patience and enthusiasm;
with a special mention for my lovely wife Shi Kai.

To the people of Nevis who offered us their hospitality, and a gift of inestimable worth : their friendship.

To those whose names may have been omitted; you will live on in our memory.

Jérôme de Baecque.